What's Your S

MW00723535

Visionary

Nadia Francois

Contributing Authors:

Nicole D. Scott, Feleshia B. Young, Vuyanzi, Tammy Boone, Laurinda Adunjar, Treva Brown, Enola Pillard, Dionne Smith, Erin Porche', Tosha Mills, Nadia Francois

Published by

Cultivate Press

Cultivate Press

Metairie, Louisiana

What's Your Super Power?
© 2020 by Nadia Francois

For Bulk Ordering and Press Inquiries
Nadia Francois
13379 Jackson Rd
Zachary, LA 70791
225-286-9053
info@whatsuperpower.com

ISBN 978-0-9910648-6-1 Paperback Print
Library of Congress Control Number: 2020917091

Imprint of Tonia Askins International LLC
1-866-553-8746

www.cultivatepress.com
Printed in the United States of America

Table of Contents

Intro

This anthology is a collection of stories from strong Black women projecting strength and resilience while overcoming life's hurdles. The purpose of this book is to showcase the many powers of a woman, encouraging other women to push through adversity to purpose. In this book the authors answer the question: What is your super power? We will share our experience when our super power is activated and the connection with God when operating in that space. We will examine the importance of faith and obedience when walking in purpose and explain the importance of a personal relationship with God. We, as women, are truly blessed with special powers from God and it is important to tap into that realm. God is blessing us for our obedience and for spreading the word about his goodness.

A Visionary, Walking By Faith

Nadia Francois

A Visionary, Walking by Faith

"Where there is no prophetic vision the people cast off restraint, but blessed is he who keeps the law.'

Proverbs 29:18 NKJV

Throughout our lives we are faced with adversity, struggles and pain, but as we grow in God we discover that most of it is a test that produces our testimony. As we walk this journey of life as Christians, it is important to connect with the Savior. We do this through faith, "the substance of things hoped for and the evidence of things not seen." (Hebrews 11:1KJV) **Faith for me is believing and living that our expectations of Christ will come into fruition.** At times, keeping the faith is difficult, but we must know and understand that faith is what helps us make it through, it is light in our dark paths, it is strength when we are weak, and without it we are nothing. Faith is our connection to God in all spiritual realms; it replenishes abundance in our heart and spirit. When we think positively and expect the best that is what we receive. Faith guides us through life and allows us to discover our purpose. A personal relationship with God is very important in discovering our purpose and establishing salvation. **He extends unwavering love and compassion towards us and views our shortcomings and setbacks only as lessons of life.** "For God so loved the world that he gave his one and only Son, that whoever believes in him shall not perish but have eternal life" (John 3:16 NKJV). This scripture holds truth to the unconditional love God has for us and the purpose that he placed on our lives at conception. We were born to win and it is our responsibility to make sure that we know, understand, and work toward this. Having a personal relationship with God and having faith the size of a mustard seed can bring us through anything.

Another important step in obtaining our purpose is obedience to God's instructions through our faith walk. **Obedience opens up a supernatural provision for us and everyone attached to us.** Sometimes the instructions make no sense to us or go against our flesh, but if it is the voice of God talking, you will know it and you will reap the reward for being obedient. Peace and joy will overflow in your life and you will be blessed greatly. In those times at adversity and uncertainty, trust God and activate your super power. What is your super power? It is your God given gift of overcoming. Whatever the trait, it brings you out of troubled water. It gives you confidence and faith that you will make it. My super power is my vision and forward thinking. I have the ability to not let the small things get in my way. The word NO is actually YES to me because I'm able to see the absolute good in everything, even when it looks grim. Philippians 3:13 says not that even though I have not attained it yet, Forgetting those things that are behind me, and pressing forward towards the mark. I am able to foreshadow and think ahead, laser focused in my yet handling every situation with grace and fortitude. I am a visionary and innovator for the kingdom and I embrace it and value it. **My life has been no picnic but my faith and my obedience to God have carried the weight for me.**

I remember going through my divorce, which was a traumatic experience for me. I was out of touch with my savior, lost, not knowing which way to turn. I couldn't go to my family or friends, fearing their judgment, so I turned to the only help I know, the good Lord. I began speaking and crying out to God for help and direction in what to do. I was twenty-eight years old with four sons, a single parent with no support from their father. When he divorced me, he divorced them as well and I think that hurt more than anything. It was during this time that I learned the power of prayer and obedience to the Father. I would put my face on when I had to face the world, but at home I was crying out pleading for relief and strength to keep going for my kids. I went through a brief depression and rebellion period. I didn't care about anyone's feelings, what they were going through, or even why they were in my life. In my prayers, I asked God to remove these feelings from my heart and he did just that. He sent me to read up on divorce and the process of grieving. I learned that everything that I was experiencing was a part of the grieving process. Grief does not only occur when someone passes away, but in any type of loss. Once I gained this important piece of information, my healing began. I then began to ask God to show me how I would raise four sons by myself, an only child with a limited support system, limited resources, and no support from their father. He told me, "Take care of your children and I will take care of you." Still uneasy but reassured, I put things in perspective and began doing just that. At the time of my divorce, my sons were the ages six, five, and one years old and super busy. Of course raising kids is no picnic, married or not, but I had my work cut out for me. Trusting and consulting the Lord along the way, he sent every provision we needed before we could request it. He put people in place to help me and my kids. We did not miss a meal or ever have to deal with being evicted or in the dark. He showered us with blessings that we could not have even dreamed of. He knew the matters of my heart aligned with the matters of his heart and he blessed me for it. He began to direct me into my purpose of empowering and uplifting women that are going through the same things that I was. As a licensed hair stylist, practicing in a low income area, I have encountered hundreds of women to encourage and tell about our Father. My ministry began behind the chair and I am forever grateful. I later started a nonprofit organization that empowers women through education, sisterhood and community outreach. This began right in my salon with a few of my clients and dear friends. On Friday nights, we had "Freaky Fridays" where I and my late crew of clients would have drinks, food and sisterly conversations about real life. The realizations and mysteries of life that were revealed to us were so refreshing and uplifting, we wanted to share this with others, so I started SiStars of Empowerment Social Organization. The name originated from most of our startup members who were also Eastern Star sisters, so we added in the "A". Our mission was to empower the women and the youth to succeed. We implemented several programs and outreach events in South Louisiana and we strive to reach women across the world. The mission became more focused on the outreach and uplifting of women because we realized that if the mother is broken, then the child is broken so we narrowed our focus. This was a vision that God is fulfilling through me and I take it very seriously. He has not given me a vision without the provision and I am tremendously grateful. Moving forward with Sistars of Empowerment, God has allowed us to be able to mentor and uplift women and girls by offering book scholarships to graduating high school seniors and start-up assistance to women entrepreneurs. I never imagined the vision of "Sistars Helping Sistars" growing into such an impactful organization. I actually never imagined having the time let alone the heart to empower other women as I am going through so much. It is in my pain that I find strength and encouragement for myself and others. I know this is God's plan because the operation and development literally just falls in place every time, no matter what. My steps are ordered and I do my best at being obedient even when I don't know the outcome.

When God gives me a vision, the execution is effortless and I can tell that I am operating in His grace and excellence. This feeling encourages me to finish what I start and to not look for worldly rewards, but the rewards of the Father. God is so good and his mercy endures forever and forever shall I walk with Him. This is not an easy walk because the world does not understand it. I have been ridiculed, lied on, and lied to but God never left me nor ridiculed me. His purpose for my life has affected me far greater and I am thankful. My super power is being a visionary, an innovator and a creator of new things. It is assigned to me by God and I am honored to carry the weight. It may seem easy to others but it is not. The obedience and discipline that is required is sometimes unbearable, but I continue to pray for strength and guidance from our Father and he continues to guide me and protect me. He allows my gifts to make room for me. The fact that I have been able to raise my four sons alone and we never missed a beat is a testimony in itself. Then he gives me the responsibility to empower women to know their worth, build their confidence and help them establish independence through entrepreneurship. He is amazing. It is my prayer that every reader of this anthology is blessed with an open mind to receive their superpower and walk in it. It's your birth right.

Therefore you are no longer a slave, but a son; and if a son, then an heir through God. – Galations 4:7 (NKJV)

What's Your Super Power

Perfect Strength
Nicole D. Scott

Perfect Strength

"...My grace is sufficient for you, for My strength is made perfect in weakness."

2 Corinthians 12:9a

Everyone wants to escape any form of weakness. No one wants to experience power in weakness. If we remove the experiences that are presented in moments of weakness by the masses, the message must be distorted — and often, it is. Two things are lost by distorting the message to make it more immediately appealing:

1.	The purity of strength is lost.

2.	The chance to embrace the beauty of becoming that is only found in adversity is lost.

My life has not been cut from a cloth of perfection. In fact, I believe I've made more mistakes and had more setbacks than most. Some of those mistakes and setbacks have been a result of my own willful ignorance and some have been because of the call of God on my life. In retrospect, life has taught me to celebrate the grace that's aligned with each step I've taken on my journey. As the oldest of four siblings, I have always been placed at the forefront. This is a blessing and a curse. Life has taught me so much over the course of the past year. I've discovered that strength is a quality everyone possess in some capacity. It took some time, life experiences, and failed relationships for me to learn that not all strength is worth celebrating. There are strong folks who are defiant in all forms of error and pride for the purpose of upholding what they deem to be right. **What if I told you strength is not strength until it's been broken?** You see, the challenge with the demand to remain strong is that so many people fight the brokenness necessary to embrace perfected strength. *This is my superpower*! Once I learned that my strength was more valuable, treasured, and complete in a broken form it became easier for me to live a surrendered life.

Everyone wants to make a success of life, but how you interpret success is of great importance. There are many people who started out in life with high ideals and a clear vision of their goals, but the unexpected pressures of life made them hard and loveless. Dependent upon their own strength, they have become calloused and cold. I became a single mom at the age of 23. I remember the tense and paralyzing conversation on the ride home from Southeastern University with my mom like it was yesterday. I remember feeling as if my entire world had come to an end. I was terrified and hopeless, all at the same time. I remember attending church throughout my pregnancy and being treated as if I had some incurable disease, simply because I was pregnant outside of marriage. Life was hard. Religious folk were mean. I was in the midst of family but isolated at the same time. I wanted to die. In fact, I recall attempting to take my life while pregnant.

Thank God the attempt failed! This was the beginning of the breaking for me. A breaking that uncovered my weaknesses. **These weaknesses, which I thought were the demise of my purpose, became the greatest tool for propelling me into purpose.** God's purpose in brokenness is to deal with the independent nature that is bent away from Him in order that a person may fulfill God's great purpose for his/her life. I had a lot of things in me that were bent away from God.

During this period of my life people around me saw strength. They saw only what I showed them as strength because I refused to allow anyone to see me broken. On the inside, I was literally walking dead. I had so many unanswered questions. I was distraught over what I thought was an abrupt end to my college career. I had to navigate daily through feelings of failure and shame. Silently, there was a ticking time bomb of anger inside of me, ready to explode. Not everything goes the way we pray or believe sometimes. At times, our expectations end in disappointment instead of victory. Sadly, we don't spend enough time on our journey of faith, self-examining and reflecting on the highlight reels of our disappointment. As a result, we have a generation of people who believe that faith is never supposed to bring disappointments, setbacks, or grief. These are the individuals who, in most cases, lose their hope in God after one hardship. One thing you must have in order to claim any form of superpower, as a believer, is stick-toitiveness. It's a MUST! Discouragement comes when people feel they have seen it all and most of it was really terrible! No matter what age you are, you have never seen it all.

On an extremely hot day in March or April of 2001, I packed all of my clothes into a hanging bag, after my mom and I had a huge argument, and struck out walking down Prescott Rd. I may have been about five months pregnant at that time. I was so infuriated about my situation that I imploded. I collapsed on the sidewalk and when I came to, I was in the back of an ambulance. Part of the beauty of God's all sufficient grace in our mess is that He comes in to rescue us from the work of our own hands, even when we don't deserve to be rescued. God saw this present day at a time when I couldn't see past that paralyzing moment. I am so grateful for the opportunity and gift of motherhood. Being a mom changed my life in the most humbling way.

We often run the risk of scaling God down to the limits of our own thoughts. Often, if we cannot see how something might happen, we convince ourselves that it won't happen. All human knowledge is fragmented, but when you learn to surrender your concepts, thoughts, ideas, and will in exchange for God's will, you give God permission to do the miraculous according to your faith. Inner resources, personal strength, creative purpose, ingenuity, natural politeness towards people, and a spirit that is sensitive to the leading of God are all qualities that reflect God's gift of grace to us. In order to grow in the spirit of God and walk in the full measure of your purpose, you must integrate each of these qualities throughout every phase your life. In your process, you have to be prepared to embrace the depth that comes from a journey where perfected strength can be found.

If you are like me or anyone else for that matter, you don't like processes or anything that has a drawn-out procedure. As much as I love my gift of administration, I hate paperwork. I don't like automated phone lines. I don't like waiting for return calls nor attending countless meetings before seeing any form of productivity or goal achieved. I just want things to happen. I especially want them to happen swiftly when it's something I have petitioned God for and labored in prayer concerning that thing for a long period of time. The times when I was the most anxious about the end result of a matter were the times when I did not want to accept the process.

You can't change where you have been, but you can change where you are going. All of my life I have had tremendous compassion for people who are hurting. I have always considered myself to be a champion for the under-dogs in life. Perhaps, it is because I've had my own pain. When you have suffered, it makes you more relatable to other people's pain. I charge you to step over any adversity you are experiencing. Instead of wasting another second agonizing over your tragedies, you should celebrate the victory of making it this far!

In closing, there is a popular song performed by gospel artists from Hillsong, to Maranda Curtis, to William Murphy and the lyrics are simple. If you know it, sing it with me.

"You are my strength.
Strength like no other.
Strength like no other.
Reaches to me.

19

In the fullness of Your grace.

In the power of Your name

You lift me up

You lift me up, let's say

Unfailing love

Stronger than mountains

Deeper than oceans

Reaches to me (in the fullest of Your grace)

In the fullness of Your grace

In the power of Your name

You lift me up

You lift me up

You are my strength.

Strength like no other.

Strength like no other.

Reaches to me."

Your strength is limited. God's strength is unlimited. Your strength is finite. God's strength is infinite. Your strength is exhaustible — that's why you get exhausted! God's strength is inexhaustible. **Sometimes, the wisdom that is the hardest to hear is the most helpful.** So, I'll

close with a strong dose of truth. There are no quick fixes. Accept that wisdom prepares us to work patiently and persistently through any process and never give up. So many experiences can injure us, keep us from stepping out, and moving ahead, but that's not the end of your story. Pray this prayer with me: *Lord God, please give me patience with the process that comes with living and strength to do the hard work that comes with choosing brokenness over my plans. I want to engage fully in the plan You have for me. You are my strength, Lord. I thank you for your strength."*

What's Your Super Power

The Empath

Laurinda Audinguar

The Empath

"When I die, burn my body. I don't want to be buried. I have spent too much time lying down."

- Frida Kahlo

E mpathy is my super power! You may have heard the term empathy used on more than a few occasions. In the event that you haven't, Meriam Webster defines empathy as "the action of understanding, being aware of, being sensitive to, and vicariously experiencing the feelings, thoughts, and experience of another of either the past or present without having the feelings, thoughts, and experience fully communicated in an objectively explicit manner."

Now that we have discussed the meaning of empathy, I have a question for you. Have you ever heard someone state that she or he is an empath? Yes?... No?... Maybe? Even if you did hear the phrase, it is possible that you did not fully understand what it truly means, nor the enormous pull that it has on an empath's psyche and emotional wellbeing, in general.

Empathguide.com describes an empath as "A person who can psychically tune in to the emotional experience of a person, place or animal. In the paranormal and in some works of science fiction and fantasy, highly developed empathy is a psychic ability to sense the emotions of others and often highly aware of the health and state of mind of their loved ones, no matter how physically near or far away the individuals may be. It can be challenging for empaths to function healthily in society if they are unaware that they have this sensitivity and often opt to be alone." I know what you are thinking, this is spooky! I get it, honestly, I do.

Please indulge me for just a moment. Empaths, like anyone else, desire to be loved. We desire to be accepted, and we desire to be contributing members of society. We hurt, we laugh, we cry, we succeed, and we fail miserably. In fact, one of my favorite quote's states "You haven't lived until you have experienced every emotion known to man in the course of a single day." (unknown) Many people would label a person who encounters that many emotions in such a short window of time crazy, unstable, or even make the assumption that they are bipolar, yet an empath experiences this daily with the added bonus of the emotional leakage of others.

Who are empaths and what do they look like? Empaths look like you and me! Also, empaths are people who may or may not have dealt with trauma themselves (however most empaths that I have encountered have experienced at least one type of trauma), which enables them to be more sensitive to the plight of others.

My name is Laurinda Andujar and I am an empath. At an early age, I knew I was different. Unfortunately, I didn't know if I was a good different or a bad different, all that I did know, was that I being different, longed to see others healthy, happy, and whole. As a child, and late into my adulthood, it devasted me to see others in pain. I would sometimes cry at the drop of a dime, and to some I appeared overly sensitive, to others, possibly a cry baby. There were times that I couldn't explain the weight of the emotions that I felt, and sometimes I thought I'd crumble under the pressure and longed for relief or at least an explanation.

I, at a young age. dealt with childhood trauma such as molestation, separation anxiety, low self-worth issues, bullying and more. Yet and still, I always stood for the underdog. For some reason, I guess I felt it was my responsibility to protect them, and try I did.

I offered my last to those who probably had more than I. I loved without limits, while at times feeling unloved. I willingly put the needs of others before my own. I was a protector. I am a protector, and I forever will be a ...protector. I once said that adversity is not your nemesis, but your adversary, and out of adversity some of the greatest heroes are born, as well as some of the strongest heroes die.

We die to self to lift the dreams and spirits of others. We lift them on broken wings of our failures and disappointments and we move in the stillness of the darkness so that they may experience the shimmer of the sun. I often found myself in a quiet space reflecting on the past, and what I could have done more of, less of, or differently concerning life in general. In those moments, you would never catch me dwelling on things that were self-serving; everything that kept me up late at night was always for the benefit of others.

I would dance the dance of the what ifs, and that dance would leave me wounded, especially if I felt that I was powerless to spare someone the bitterness associated with the disappointments of life. I remember watching a 2008 film directed by Gina Prince-Bythewood, and executive produced by Jada Pinkett-Smith, titled "The Secret Life of Bees". The movie was eerily relatable to me. It had an impressive star-studded cast which consisted of veteran actors such as Queen Latifah, Jennifer Hudson, Dakota Fanning, Paul Bettany, Nate Parker, Alicia Keys, Sophie Okonedo and others.

Even though the film was filled to the brim with so many talented actors, there was one character in particular played flawlessly by Sophie Okonedo that drew me in, who held my heart hostage at hello. The character's name was Mae Boatwright, at first glance, she was nothing out of the ordinary, she was odd... simple. Mae was in her mid to late twenties, but she had an innocent child-like nature about her. Mae would be full of glee and springing with life in the moment and in a split second, she would be drenched in a cape of sorrow. In the end, she ended up committing suicide because she could no longer bare the afflictions that the world graciously bestowed upon her.

No one could unravel the complexity of her personage, yet to me it was simple. I recognized the signs. It was written all over her fabric. The trauma that she experienced through the passing of her twin had become her strength and her kryptonite all in one. The death left her open, naked before the world, and the world was callous and cruel. It was as if I was watching my life unfold on screen and could do nothing to help her.

I wanted to scream, I see you sis, I am here for you! I wanted to embrace her and straighten her crown. I wanted her to know that she was bigger than any struggle and that she mattered. I wanted her to know that she was not a mistake and that she was going to be okay. I wanted her to know that everything around her could be in shambles, but her current situation had no bearing on how God would use her. I wanted her to realize how amazing she was. I saw it, why couldn't she see it?

I recall a quote that read "broken crayons still color." I wanted her to know that her brokenness, her flaws, her quirks are what made her beautiful. I wanted her to know that I could relate to the barrenness of being broken.

I came from what some would call a broken home. However, to me, nothing was broken, it was the norm, mind you to me it was the normal because *my norm* was all I knew. I was raised by a single, hardworking and honest mother. She sacrificed to give us the life she never had. My father was absent for the most part, and he was equally as toxic in his presence. I was the typical, walking, talking, and breathing stereotype. All things considered I was happy and I was loved.

Thinking back on my childhood, I am the person I am today because of my mother. She always looked out for us and others. She made sure that if someone was hungry, they had a hot meal. If they had no money, she would make sure they had exactly what they needed to be more comfortable. She always provided a listening ear. She was a problem solver and she always seemed to be in tune with others. She ALWAYS placed a high priority on the care and concern for others.

It was her ability to place herself in the shoes of others that always captivated me. I would study her. I studied her so much, that I began to think like her. I felt connected to her on a deeper level. I could feel her joy. I could feel her pride, and I could feel her pain. The intensity of it at times was debilitating, almost crippling. Even to this day, I will get a "feeling" and I will not be at peace until I hear her voice or see her, and nine times out of ten, those feelings were spot on. I was in tune with her.

I was vibing on her frequency you could say. The interesting thing is that the more time that I spent not only with my mom, but others, I found myself in tune with their emotions as well. I vividly remember instances of being at work and not being able to focus because someone smiled, however what I felt was contrary to what I saw.

I would ask a question and disclose an intimate detail about them that I had no awareness of how I knew it or where it came from, and then the tears would begin to flow. I would then find myself assuring said person that it would be okay and end up hugging it out or attempting to help them work through the problem. Almost always I would reach out to a peer or mentor that could provide the tangible tools that were needed to move them along in their transition.

Enter the Grief Recovery Institute, I knew there had to be more out there and I knew there just had to be a reason that I felt compelled to leave people better than I found them. No, I do not have a God complex, it's the God that I serve that convicts me to love on people. It was He, who ensured that all of the pain and trauma that I experienced would not go wasted. My pain was purposefully instrumental in my pursuit to spread healing.

I have met many wonderful empaths along my journey and each one of them also full of purpose have provided a missing piece of the puzzle to assist me with gaining the resources that I needed to be effective. One of the most effective tools that I was able to place in my toolbelt, was the gift of the knowledge of grief recovery. All of my life, I had been walking around aimlessly, with the lingering effects of trauma. I reacted to everything from an injured perspective.

I was sad, beat up and barren. I could not handle my emotions let alone someone else's, I longed for something… anything to relieve the pressure. So, I set out on a trek to become a grief recovery specialist. (GRS). I truly thought I was going to learn how to assist others with walking through their pain. Little did I know, it was the biggest setup for my come up… emotionally. I should have known that it was going to be intense. I walked in the classroom and the rules were simple:

- Respect the privacy of others
- Do not compare your losses
- Do not attempt to fix anyone
- Avoid alcohol, smoking or your usual numbing agent of choice… WE WANT YOU TO FEEL EVERYTHING!

Feel? I didn't come here to feel anything. Feelings were in my opinion, the kryptonite that caused the majority of my issues in life, or so I thought. To be honest I was tired of feeling. I just wanted to know how to fix others, so that I could … feel better. There goes that feeling word again. All of my adulthood I was taught that no one really cared about or wanted to really hear how I felt. Then there I was in the middle of "feely" central. I was mortified.

I wanted to run, and I might have considered it had I not spent a small fortune attempting to learn how to assist others navigate through the murky waters called grief. I am glad that I had the fortitude to see the training through until the end (that and the fact that I am extremely cheap), I will never be able to make sense of wasting money, but I digress.

Anyway, here I am in the middle of feely central and for the first time in my life I have a solid understanding on what grief is and how it affects us all differently. One of the most critical things that I learned over the course of my training at the Grief Recovery Institute was the fact that "grief is a person's natural response to a loss." Another thing that I learned that was equally as important, is that we all deploy avoidance tactics when it comes to handling grief. I mean who **wants** to deal with painful issues?

I can recall a time that I was grieving the loss of a relationship and I attempted to get drunk to. I wanted desperately to feel better, so I drank two entire bottles of wine and nothing happened, I could no longer get numb. I was forced in that moment to deal with the assault of emotions that were invading my mental space, and I didn't like it one bit. In that moment I realized that I was like many of the people that I talked with daily. I was a griever.

Had I not had a lifeline to reach out to, I may not have been here to share this story with you today. I was blessed to have someone in the moment that understood the difference between enabling and empowering.

With that being said, one of the biggest challenges that I would now have to overcome is making sure I had not become an enabler to those who were brave enough to pull themselves out of the quicksand of pity and self-loathing. Believe me, this happens easier than one would care to admit. Being an empath is all about the ability to relate and make connections for the common good without creating casualties.

Fade to black, this is the moment in the story line where the unlikely hero learns of her true strength and what she was created for. It is in this moment of training and vulnerability where strength is uncovered through every broken bone, every stripe, every torn muscle, every tear, every loss finally makes sense. Empathy is her superpower and she is no longer afraid to use it and in 2015, I did just that.

I founded Heal the City Incorporated and years later in 2018 I was granted my 5013c charitable organization status, under the name of Heal the City Incorporated. The mission of Heal the City Inc is to have candid conversations and bring awareness on tough issues such as rape, molestation, suicide, domestic violence, grief and other topics to heal the world one city at a time. I founded HTC Inc. because I saw an alarming trend in at risk communities where resources such as counseling, mentoring and development programs were scarce, but the demand was great.

Since our Inaugural event in March of 2016, Heal the City has touched many individuals internationally and domestically in hopes of creating positive outlets in a safe and collaborative environment. Heal the City is not about having the next big star on stage, HTC is about making an impact. We want people to know that they are never alone, and that we are more alike than we are different.

I have invested a lot of time and energy in finding the right people to share their stories. It was extremely important that the Mae Boatwrights in attendance felt not only safe enough to approach our speakers, but would allow themselves to be vulnerable enough to get naked before them to seek help they need. I wanted our speakers, coaches and professionals to demonstrate that anyone can overcome if they have the right mindset, tools and desire to change.

I wanted people in my corner who shared the same love for people as I did. I wanted people who would rock the boat in a good way. I wanted people who were not afraid to jump overboard to save the life of another. I wanted people who were comfortable enough in their skin to speak of their battle with trauma, yet not be consumed by it.

I wanted people who were like quality pitchers; willing to pour out to fill others and solid enough to stand the cycles of constant use. In short, I needed people who believed in their craft enough to stay current and relevant, all in the hopes of planting seed into the lives of others.

I wanted people in my corner whose heart breaks for what breaks God's heart. I wanted people who knew firsthand what it felt like to be unloved, unnoticed, unappreciated and unapologetically flawed. I wanted people in my corner who walked through the fire and have yet to lose the respect for the scars that heat produced. I wanted people in my corner whose vibrations were so high that it forced whomever that chanced to come into their presence to level up.

I am proud to say that God has granted me all of those requests. I am not going to say that the road to healing was easy, but what I can say, without a shadow of a doubt, is that being an empath on this journey, made it all the more worthwhile.

What's Your Super Power

Passion Purpose Prayer

Enola Pillard

Passion Purpose Prayer

M y superpower is walking as a woman with passion, purpose and prayer. As a young girl, I always had ambition. In high school, when there was homecoming, sleepovers, prom, and dances, I was always the one doing everyone's hair. Before I knew it, I was doing hair in a room at my mom's house. Reading magazines and watching videos gave me great interest in becoming a cosmetologist. After graduating from high school, listening to other girls going to school to be doctors, lawyers, teachers and social workers, I felt different. I really was thinking something was wrong with me for wanting different. For two years, I tried other things and actually went to school and worked different jobs. For some strange reason, I felt empty and incomplete. I would always go to my mom for advice. No matter how hard I tried, this feeling wouldn't go away. She advised me to pray and use wisdom. She was teaching me how to be independent and make decisions on my own. As I approached womanhood, my life was changing. **Through prayer, the answer I received was to follow my passion, to do what I love to do** and that was being a hairstylist. Passion is defined as a feeling that you can recognize as being very intense. I recognize every leader view passion as a key to success, so I begin to write my vision and discovering my next steps. That step was to become a professional cosmetologist, I had to go to school. I realize it was nothing wrong with being different. What is for me, is for me. It's great to have an idea, but you have to recognize the time to take action. Making school a priority was one of the best decisions I ever made. I am now 25 years strong as a licensed cosmetologist and a licensed cosmetology instructor. I'm so grateful I took wise counsel from my mom. If I told you it was easy it wasn't, but with determination and self-discipline, I stayed focus. We are all born with gifts, talents and special abilities. Passion will give you the strive and drive to become successful. Allowing passion to become the blueprint, map and compass that will lead you on the path to your destiny.

As I journey through life, I realize nothing I've experienced was in vain. Every achievement and accomplishment was connected to my divinely designed purpose in life. Looking at the woman in the mirror, I wondered how I can make a change. I had to no longer allow my past, failures and mistakes to hold me back. I had to, once and for all, deal with my insecurities that held me back. Picking up the pace realizing every challenge was to draw me closer to my purpose. I never imagined being a single mom, but from being a single mom, I realized I can inspire other single moms. By sharing testimonies and stories that I've overcome, I may help someone else. I strive with a made up mind that I can and will walk in purpose. Sometimes, you will never know what you are made of until you overcome. It's amazing how God works things out for your good. Walking on the road called purpose, I was not alone. God was with me all the time. Knowing through Christ we can do all things. One day after church a young lady walked up to me sharing how she watch me all the time. She thanked me for being an example of a strong women. I was so glad that God's light was shining through me.

Through much prayer and supplication, I made it this far by faith. As a young girl, I would always see my grandmother praying. Growing up as an adult, I applied prayer to my own life. Things I've overcome without a doubt, I could not take the credit. Only by God's grace, I've made it this far. Prayer is the way I communicate with God. In Jeremiah 29:11, it says, there is a hope and future for me. God has a hope and future for me? Just knowing that fills my heart with joy and gladness. In prayer, as I bow before the throne of grace, in faith to my creator, the one that holds my world in his hands, gives me comfort and peace. I pray daily for guidance and direction, confident that my steps will be ordered by the Lord. Letting my heart not be troubled, knowing he will give me peace in the time of trouble. Seeing miracles, signs and wonders, I know he hears my prayers. Through prayer, I've gained a personal relationship with God. Learning his voice and feeling his presence builds my faith to hold on to his unchanging hand. My grandmother has gone home to be with the Lord. I wish I could thank her for teaching me how to pray. As I read in the Bible about the Proverbs 31 woman, I learned to be a virtuous women. She was a woman walking with passion, purpose, and prayer. She walked boldly with integrity, a woman that we can admire. Applying what God has identified as my superpower- passion, purpose and prayer, I will join other trailblazers and forerunners in this world as God's leading ladies.

What's Your Super Power

Faith Over Fear, Navigating Uncharted Paths

Dr. Treva Tarnese Brown

Faith Over Fear, Navigating Uncharted Paths

W hen confronted with the question, "What is my superpower?", I must first give you a glimpse of how much mentoring and encouragement it takes from family, friends, and faculty to guide a young girl from Baton Rouge, LA down a path from first generation college student, through undergraduate school, to graduate school, leading to my current career path as a scientist. You see, I know what it is like to feel less than confident and to feel like you don't see a place for yourself in the vast realm of career options and male dominated spaces. My story resounds the old saying, "it takes a village" to help someone discover the paths less traveled.

As a teenager, I never knew exactly what career path I wanted to follow once I finished high school. My becoming a scientist happened because of a chain of experiences led by my faith and belief that God would guide my decisions and footsteps. I believe He helped others to see my potential, and in turn they showed me a mirror with a hazy reflection at the start of my journey. That hazy image turned out to be me, Dr. Treva T. Brown, who's superpower resulted from those that believed in me.

One of my most memorable hurdles I faced through my career path happened as I was trying to matriculate through my undergraduate institution. I was struggling in my Physics class, and it was suggested to me that I change majors so I could graduate "on time". There were even three different degree options laid out for me, and I was told that I had to pick one. That moment was like a blurred, slow motion tract where my thoughts overrode the words being spoken to me. Thanks to my amazing support system, all I could do was picture my family and friends that believed in me. At that moment, I gathered the printed degree options and boldly exclaimed, "I'm graduating from LSU with a degree in Chemistry, just watch me!", and I left the office.

After this encounter, I immediately went to one of my mentor's office, and he reminded me that I came to LSU with the determination to get a degree in the field I had chosen, which was chemistry. He asked if I still loved chemistry, and when I confirmed, he asked, '…you've worked hard to get to this point, so what's the difference now? Because someone told you that you couldn't do it? What do YOU think about graduating in chemistry?" I responded that I believed I could do it. He said calmly, "well, you need to dry up all those tears and do it. Remember, that's why we're here to help you."

Because of my mentors as well as my parents being the leading force behind my strong support system, I not only refused the advisor's advice, but I also made it through the most difficult point in my college career. Now, I could clearly see that I was beginning to walk in my purpose, guided by my religious beliefs and my faith in God. I was encouraged to write my first scientific article as an undergraduate, which got published! I was winning all kinds of awards and traveling to conferences to present my research. It was insane! I finally found my wings and a career path. Can you imagine the blessings I would have missed out on if I listened to the nay-sayers?

So what is my purpose in sharing this story with you? Think about the times where people said you couldn't do something. Think about the times when people turned their back on you because you weren't following the path they laid out for your life? Think about the times where this negativity discouraged you and caused you to lose your faith in pursuing your dream. We've all been there. However, it is my purpose to share this story with you to tell you that those nay-sayers, those negative people in your life - they are only the devil's roadblock to tempt you to lose sight of the goals you've already prayed about. Simply take a moment, step back, reach out to those who have your best intentions at heart, and PRAY yourself through it. Trust me, you'll sit back and reminisce, as I am doing in my story, and think about all of the turning points in your life that allowed you to reach beyond the dream that you were working to attain. It is in this moment that you will too discover your superpower.

As for me, I always tell people, my journey wasn't an easy road by any stretch of the imagination and I still have roads yet to travel. **In my graduate school career, I almost quit three times.** The first time, I wasn't producing the results I needed. But God placed a postdoctoral student in my path who sat me down in my office and told me that there was something about me that was different and unique. She explained that if I hung in there, I would have something that I could share with others like myself. In turn, I told my parents that I wanted to try harder before I gave up. The second time, God allowed my parents to hug me so tight and reassure me that I could make my dreams come true if I continued to trust in and put my faith in God. This is also when my spiritual walk with God got even deeper. By the third time I second guessed myself, my parents just said, 'you are in this to stay now!" And that's when my community, my mentors, my family and friends seemed to uplift me every day and remind me that I was achieving a dream that many never even fathom achieving. My drive and determination to continue was also fueled by the fact the younger generation, especially young girls, needed to see representation of a scientist that looked like them and worked in their community.

As the popular saying goes, 'Nevertheless she persisted...", and persisted I did indeed. I remember the day my graduate research advisor called me wanting to know if I had started looking for jobs as I was nearing the end of my Ph. D. candidacy. A scientist from the U.S. Naval Research Laboratory at NASA's Stennis Space center had reached out to him asking about my microscopy skills because they had a position opening up. Long story short, this same once shy young girl from Baton Rouge, LA, was being sought after for her contributions to chemistry in the field of microscopy. I will never forget that day when I was offered the position of physical scientist for the U.S. Naval Research Laboratory. It was amazing! Later that evening, I found out that I was selected for a National Award for Leadership from the National Organization of Black Chemists and Chemical Engineers. In my mind, it was all too good to be true because it had been so difficult for me up to that point. But I credit none other but God!

I did it! I walked across the stage with my Doctorate in Chemistry from the University of New Orleans in December 2017! Today, I am one of few females and the only African American Ph. D. scientist in my section at work. Hopefully my story can serve as motivation to those who, like myself, didn't know where to start and wasn't sure of how to navigate unchartered territory to achieve goals and dreams once perceived unattainable.

Now that you've read my story, can you guess what my superpower may be? My answer… my superpower is TENACITY. Without my God-given superpower of tenacity, I would not be who nor where I am today. A personal relationship with God is a journey that every individual will experience in different capacities. For me, my personal relationship with God helped fuel my tenacity to continue pushing through my personal hurdles. **Daily, I take comfort in knowing that God will order my steps and fight my battles seen and unseen.** Therefore, I tend to stress less, enjoy life more, and I can truly say that I am happy. I pray that my story has encouraged and motivated you to stay the course, trust in your faith, and believe in yourself always. Remember, with faith, you can move mountains!

"...if you have faith as small as a mustard seed, you can say to this mountain, 'Move from here to there,' and it will move. Nothing will be impossible for you." –
Matthew 17:20

What's Your Super Power

Forgiveness Gave Me Life

Tammy Boone

Forgiveness Gave Me Life

When I decided to be a part of this superpower anthology, I honestly struggled with identifying my superpower. One, because we are our own worst critic, right? Well, that can be due in part to the fact that we gauge ourselves based upon the trickery of comparison. Comparing our looks, style, success, significant other, diction, friendships, car, home, education, and employment status to others which over time can lead to a voiceless assassination. Not in actual meaning, but in a grudge-causing, dream-squashing, and panic-triggering kind of way. In other words, it is an assassination that has the potential to eradicate your self-worth based solely on falsely perceived standards. Two, how do you determine a superpower? Is it based upon what one does well or what one has mastered or is it simply based upon a pursued passion? Well, after careful thought, I decided that my superpower is an attribute that can change the entire trajectory of your life – it did for me! The superpower I am speaking of is forgiveness, more specifically, self-forgiveness. I would like to express to you in writing the liberation I experienced through the act and ask that you stick with me for a moment as I share pieces of me in an effort to liberate you as well.

Yes, I am fully aware of the buzz surrounding the topic as it has been discussed ad nauseam. However, I would like to start with its definition. Forgiveness, as defined by Webster, is ceasing to feel resentment against an offender. It is an intentional decision to let go of feelings of anger and resentment toward someone who you believe has wronged you. In other words, it is almost like a pardon where the offender is excused of an offense without penalty. While accurate in its definition, **forgiveness to me, is the act of acknowledging, accepting, and then releasing, the emotions and the mindset associated with an offense.** Now that I've explained the word forgiveness, let me define self-forgiveness. Self-forgiveness must be when one ceases to feel anger and resentment towards self. The only thing is, with self-forgiveness, instead of changing your view concerning others you will change your view concerning you. Hence, there must be a change in the emotions you feel towards you. Simply put, the way you view yourself will need to shift from resentment to approval and from anger to delight (as an example). Since I have discussed what self-forgiveness is, I would like to briefly discuss what self-forgiveness is not. It is not about letting yourself off the hook. It does not even suggest that you are condoning the behavior. Instead, it means that you accept the action, you accept the circumstance and are prepared to move forward without constantly reflecting over occurrences that cannot be changed.

I am pretty certain that we all have faced situations that required the release of an offense towards someone who offended us. We have also encountered the opposite where someone we had offended had to release us from an offense that we committed towards them. But **how often do we go through the process of forgiving ourselves - both as the offender and the offended?** Yes, I said it, you as the offender as well as the offended. Why do I say this? Because I, too, had to take a step back to figure me out. I discovered the offender to be my ruminating thoughts, which caused me to stay in a place of stuck without moving towards a resolution. As long as I was stuck, I could never walk in nor fulfill my purpose and because of that, I **became the offended.** I was offended by the paralyzing effects of my negative feelings that were nurtured in my past and were designed to keep me from my future.

So, taking two steps back while yet trying to figure me out, I realized that the only way I could crawl out of the drudge of unforgiveness was to process through rejection and abandonment (to name a few); emotions that shaped the very foundation of my origin. Let me help you to see the issue here. My past does not afford me the privilege of looking back fondly on special occasions, such as birthdays, family parties, and cherished moments of daily enjoyment like trips to the playground or snug bedtime stories. You see, I lacked the distinct and unmistakable bond shared between a mother and daughter. A bond that I never had the opportunity to experience therefore could not quite wrap my mind around the concept surrounding the evolution that takes place during the course of a mother-daughter relationship. For as beautiful as she was, so says the yellow tinted and gently faded photo hanging on the wall, I would never have the opportunity to slowly collect the breadcrumbs of her life that would have been dropped for me along the way. A guide that would unveil her secrets of womanhood. You know like, how she managed to maintain her beauty, how she kept every strand of hair in place, how she determined which lipstick to wear with what outfit, how fun her life was as a Christian, how she pushed through difficult times, how she maintained her happiness, how long she had been saved, how she and my father met, where her fashion sense originated, what kind of person she was, how she trusted God in the midst of trouble, or even how she had faith in the midst of her unbelief. Those important details would always remain a mystery as my mother passed away when I was an infant and I could only wonder what she was like based upon the relationship I held with her photo.

Strong and confident are not attributes I possessed early on in life, mainly because I had no biological father to shape nor influence those images. The presence of a father matters, however, my father was not around. He was not there to demonstrate what a good relationship (of any kind) resembled. I never saw him open a door for my mother. I never saw him pull out her chair before they were seated. I never saw him walk on the outside (to the right of her) of my mother as they strolled through the park holding hands. I never saw them sitting around the table discussing bills. I never heard them having conversations of understanding, meaning, and love. I never heard them laughing together. I never experienced us (3 siblings, myself, my mother, and father) sitting at the table having dinner as a family. I never had the opportunity to hear him picking that electric guitar in church on Sunday mornings. I never saw how a man could have a true relationship with God. I never saw how he led the family as he was led by God. I never knew how a king was supposed to treat his queen. I never had the opportunity to run in to the arms of my father as he protected me from the wiles of the world. None of those attributes were visible in my life because he wasn't visible in my life. My father did not have the capacity to care for me and therefore, simply put, he did not!

I was not only dealing with the feelings and thoughts that plagued my mind, which, by the way, governed my life, I was also trying to sift through the sieve of confusion surrounding the anguish of my parent's absence in spite of not having a memory of being in their presence. I blamed myself for everything, right down to the death of my mom and the abandonment of my father. I would often reflect on a connection that never was, for those biological parents I never had. Reflections, which over time, diminished any trace of my origin.

I was a mental mess and had grown into this raging, insecure female who sought validation, trusted unusually quick, and loved far too deep. I lived the majority of my life buried under the guise of anger, bitterness, and self-resentment. I could not stop thinking and just "be." The painful thoughts centered around the absence of my parents were on constant rewind in my mind and eventually created a mental repository of pain. As a young adult, I remember getting a glimpse of myself in a mirror, an object in which I lacked a connection. I did not like looking in mirrors because doing so forced me to become familiar with someone with whom I was not genuinely acquainted. However, on this particular morning, the glimpse turned into a piercing stare and I begin to take notice of what was staring back in my face. For the first time, I was able to identify my unrecognizably blemished shell that was skillfully clothed in insecurities, brokenness, and defeat. I was tired and mentally drained! I needed this to be fixed. NO! I needed to be fixed! I begin to pray "Create in me a clean heart, O God, and renew a right spirit within me (Psalm 51:10).

I soon realized that God was positioning me for a change. He began to deal with me about self-forgiveness. In fact, he showed me how self-forgiveness would expose the deadly toxins that covered my heart and how the exposure would eventually reveal what was on my mind through the words that flowed from my mouth (Matthew 15:18). In other words, **self-forgiveness would reveal the negative residue that had nestled in my heart and eventually act as a catalyst towards restoration.**

Now that I have shared pieces of me, I would like to briefly discuss my process and it starts with granting anger, bitterness, and self-resentment, the permission to exist temporarily. Exist long enough for me to confirm the authenticity of the feelings behind the emotions I carried. Once I verified the feelings to be true, I then had to put in the work. I had to roll up my sleeves, sling my heels to the side and dig through the murky sediments of my life. This was very critical as I needed to determine where and how the feelings formed. Standing with the roots of anger, bitterness, and self-resentment in my hand, heart, and mind, I then had to unmask the behaviors that I experienced. Now, here comes that part that people take lightly, and to me, it was not a light task at all. Once the feelings in my hand, heart, and mind were unmasked, I then had to rid myself of them by letting them go.

What is important to note here is that self-forgiveness released me from the bondage of my past and placed me on the path to identifying my authentic self, which is essentially found in Christ. Once I caught hold of that revelation, I begin to understand the "He had set me apart before I was born and called me by his grace" (Galatians 1:15) for his purpose. I could then stand firm in knowing that I was "fearfully and wonderfully made" (Psalm 139:14).

I have lived with the sense of not belonging and it has played a vital role in shaping who I have become, which is a grown woman who still deals with the effects of rejection and abandonment from time to time. I still have unanswered questions about my origin, but have come to terms with the fact that I am not my pain, my past, nor my emotions. I realized that my full potential and purpose would never show up without self-forgiveness. I abandoned self-resentment by forgiving myself for allowing negativity to drive the narrative of my life and began evolving into the person God created me to be.

Today, I chose to use my life's experiences to make a difference in others. I am reminded that, in God, there are no flaws or failures and because of this, it is easier to take a glimpse into the mirrors of my life, even if I spot a blemish or two. I implore you to choose forgiveness, choose self-forgiveness, and let the power of forgiveness liberate you as well. May the love and grace of our Lord and Savior Jesus Christ continue to be with you!

What's Your Super Power

What Lies Beneath

Vuyanzi

What Lies Beneath

I will praise You, for I am fearfully and wonderfully made;

Marvelous are Your works...

Psalm 139:14

People constantly say to me, "I love your energy!" What they don't know is that while I've always been a person with high energy, this particular energy that they see is from me accepting the beauty that is within me. My Super Power is my energy. There is a freedom and liberation I possess that produces the energy people see today. This is because I can look at myself and accept and embrace the person I am. To embrace and accept myself means that I can more readily embrace and accept you and anyone else who comes across my path. I smile because I know that I am exactly who I am supposed to be. This may sound oversimplified, however, **it took decades for me to accept me just the way I was**. The energy that they feel, the energy they see come out, the energy that I exude, is because I had to build it, piece by piece. I want to begin by getting an understanding of what energy is. Everything is energy. Energy is a vibration or frequency. The frequency that I give off is high and therefore others notice.

People are drawn to my energy even when I am not even trying. I cannot say what my energy has always come from as I am not sure what has kept my vibration high throughout my life. I have believed that it was an innate characteristic of my being. Now, at the age of 46, I have put together an equation from which I am sure my energy feeds. Just as in an addition problem, it does not matter if you switch the order, they are equal to my energy:

Vuyanzi's Energy = Passion + Spirit + Aura + Sensitivity + Positivity + Confidence + Inspiration + Humor

My passion is a big part of my Super Power because I have witnessed it to act as an invisible current from my heart to the hearts of others. When I am passionate about something, it comes across with great energy. With any

Super Power comes great responsibility, to take a piece of Uncle Ben's (no, not the rice guy, silly, I have never known him to say a thing)   quote to his nephew, Peter Parker also known as Spiderman in the movie Spiderman. "With great power comes great responsibility." I can become passionate about what I am talking about in an instant, without much prompting. Lying is not my thing, but if it were (pregnant pause here), I know that I could convince people to believe in things that are not real because of the passion I can display. I can be enthusiastic (I am using enthusiastic interchangeably with passion) about, well, nearly anything and everything that I like and I can imagine and justify. Whether it's when I speak to someone about my dog, but of course, I love him or the enthusiasm I have shown when talking to people about products I was selling for educational companies. Teachers have walked out saying, the now infamous line, "Wow, I loved your energy," while others have asked for my contact information to stay in touch and others have hugged me, yes, you read that right, but I love hugs therefore they were not creepy. This passion-induced energy continues to show up and is infectious.

Why am I so positive? Sometimes, I merely want to walk around with a sourpuss face on for a day instead of this involuntary smile that I often find on my face, even when things are awful in my life. The problem is that my spirit will not allow it. It simply will not stay in that space of despair. I believe that it is for this reason that my spirit is connected to my positivity. They are nearly twins. For some reason, I can see the silver lining in (too) many (according to me) situations. Try me, tell me about your situation and I will somehow, nearly effortlessly, find your silver lining. Some days, this feels like a curse more than a gift. Every time someone tells me some bad news, I want to encourage them with the positive side, however, I have come to understand that not every person wants to hear that. At times the person just wants someone to listen (I discovered this when a couple friends of mine asked me to shut up during a story and not tell them the positive side). My spirit of happiness is linked to this positivity and it is an attributing factor to my high vibration. A high vibration is directly connected to strong positive feelings.

Let your light so shine before men that they may see your good works and glorify your father in heaven....
Matt 5:16

"Wow, when you walked into the room you were like...Slay! Slay! Slay!" All I had done was, simply, walk into a crowded birthday party and looked for a friend. Who did I slay? (I saw no victims). This was the comment from a gentleman in attendance at the party who wanted some of the slaying energy he witnessed. On another occasion, "Queen, I loved the way you walked in here like a boss!" said a friend of mine. Huh? I, just, walked into the gym looking for him! My aura is something I truly do not understand, but I can feel my transformation into it when I walk into a crowded room.

Aura is the distinctive atmosphere or quality that seems to surround and be generated by a person, thing or place...

Most times it stems from my nervousness. I frequently walk into situations, by myself, with no familiar faces and the nerve knot hits my tummy. In that moment, I must fake it until I make it. Aura is a light that shows, and this is not to say that an actual light shows around me as a halo does on the head of an angel or does it? (Enter the furrowed brow of Columbo.) I don't think so. I have put a plan into place before leaving home for an event. I make a decision that I will have a great time regardless of who is there and what is going on. Often times, I do not know what kind of experience is awaiting me when I go into a new environment, but making a decision about the unknown has never led to disappointment.

My aura, my light, comes through whether I am at a nightclub dancing to my favorite Notorious B.I.G. song or at a fitness gym flipping over a tire. I will continue to let this light shine before men (and I guess the ladies too) because I know it is a part of my Super Power that has drawn people.

...[Jesus] He was moved with compassion for them...
Matthew 9:36

I wept uncontrollably after seeing the Pursuit of Happiness with Will Smith to the point of embarrassment. I was with my children in the movie theatre. I still cry when I watch Terms of Endearment and Beaches knowing from the beginning that one of the main characters will die. (No spoiler alerts here! These movies are old and if you have not watched them by now, forget it!) I have felt moved by the human condition of the downtrodden people that I have seen on the streets and felt completely ill-equipped to help them thus producing more sentiment for them in my heart.

As a kid, I remembered, in my family, we used to throw the phrase around, "You're so sensitive." In retrospect, it was more like saying, *why are you crying after I just hurled a bunch of insults that may or may not have hurt that I meant to hurt you, but now you're crying and I feel awkward so, "You're so sensitive" feels like the best way out of this…*

Do you get the point? My heart feels pierced easily, however, not as easily as it used to feel. Becoming a teacher, for a number of years, hardened me a bit because I couldn't always allow my heart to lead as I taught middle schoolers who can be sweet, cunning and a little sneaky sometimes. This sensitivity, I do believe I was born with and in 2006, do not ask me how I remember the year, but it is so, that I decided that being sensitive was not an inferior trait. I would embrace my sensitive self-knowing that it made me more relatable to all. **My sensitivity is the ignition for my compassion and without it, I would not be me.** This has allowed me to experience a greater sense of self which is a trait of having a high vibration too.

May I make a confession that when I finally made myself sit down to write this (all of this after debating and deliberating for, like, a year, okay, maybe it was more like two months, but it was too long), I cried. I honestly wept, like Jesus (I wasn't there when he did it, but the Bible says it so…). This is how it went down, I looked in the mirror and thought, "I am gorgeous. I am simply beautiful with my chocolatey self," and then I began to cry because I began thinking about all the times I looked at myself and I saw ugliness. A part of this equation that attributes to my Alicia Energy is my confidence. The origin of my self-confidence was birthed out of thinking I was not good enough. There were numerous times that I looked at my hair, felt its coarseness and thought it was ugly and undesirable. I looked at my cheeks, my chubby cheeks (which I, now, think of as an asset) and thinking how I wanted high cheekbones to look like my beautiful grandmother whose were distinct, but I did not have them. I have traveled a long way in my self-perception and the journey had numerous stops along the way. There was an eye-opening experience that helped me to understand the stories I told myself that contributed to my view of myself. I had this come to Jesus moment as a volunteer at my church's, at the time, youth group that opened my eyes to who I really was versus who I thought I was. Since they were in sixth grade, I wanted to make myself relatable and found one of my middle school pictures to share with them on our first meeting together. I unveiled my middle school self to my girls only sixth grade students and thought they would surely laugh hysterically saying how ugly I was, but instead, they embraced it warmly asking me about my big "afro" not understanding my chemically induced hair of the 1980s.

They did not fall off their chairs pointing at my picture, holding their bellies with uncontrollable laughter as I thought they might. Quite possibly, I had stumbled on to something, that I was not as hideous as I thought. I looked like the regular kid that I was in a school picture and that, my friends, was simply it. It was one notch in raising my beliefs in my self-perception. **It took me over three decades of my life to realize that being beautiful was a decision that I could have made long ago**. "I am gorgeous. I am simply beautiful with my chocolatey self!" I can never be anyone else except me. I came to that hard realization as I tried to be what I was not. My confidence is a direct connection to my energy. I feel good about who I am on the inside and on outside.

...stir up the gift of God which is in you... 2 Timothy 1:6

"I felt so inspired."

"You are so inspiring."

The first thoughts that used to come to my mind when I heard that I was inspiring after a speech was a black preacher in a pulpit preaching, sweating and spitting and there was decidedly nothing appealing about this to me, however, there has been a change in my view. Within the past couple of years, scratch that within the past couple of months, I have learned to embrace what I have been around my entire life. My sphere has been entrenched with charismatic gospel preachers who were, indeed, influential and inspiring including my pastor whose tutelage I was under for the majority of my life, the late Bishop Kenneth Robinson, my own grandmother, the late Evangelist Lucy P. Whitley, messenger of the gospel, pianist, ½ of my guardianship (Granddaddy was the other half) and purveyor of the belt to my behind, and my mom, Reverend Lucy (yep she's a junior) G. Rodman, gospel slinger, prayer warrior, and counselor to many. These days as she approaches 90 years old, most often she answers to the title of "Mother Rodman." With all of these influences, was it not bound to rub off? All of these people were influential in one way or another throughout my existence. Admittedly, I did not appreciate all of these influences when I was growing up, I, simply, did not want to be called inspiring. I felt it was a cop out word when people could not think of something else to say, similarly to the way "nice" is used when one wants to describe a man who isn't very attractive that she wants to hook up with a friend, not that that has ever happened to me (wink, wink). Today, I welcome being described as inspiring because I am inspired on a daily basis and with that I recognize that inspired people inspire people. One of the traits of high vibration is feeling inspired and yet another part of my energy, my Super Power.

A merry heart does good like medicine… Proverbs
17:22

Then there is my humor, that dry-ish humor. It is somehow a mix of Seinfeld meets Sanford and Son. I crack myself up every day and frequently find myself laughing so hard at my own jokes while other people may not exactly get them. My humor, I must say, is the part of my Super Power that I love to see has rubbed off on my three children. It is a way of moving positivity to the next level. It's not just about seeing the silver lining, it is about seeing the humor and even situations that are serious. Recently, my children, now adults, had a family text where we were deciding who in the family is the funniest and I am sorry to say that I, as the reigning queen, has been toppled by one of my twin boys, Aaron. All of them, keep me laughing and I keep them laughing. Laughter has helped me stay balanced in chaos and that is a trait of having a high vibration. It has helped to make bad situations more palpable; it helps to put distance between a hurtful situation and me and it helps me to gain perspective that I pass on. Having humor has taught me that when you remove yourself from a situation and look at it from a bird's eye view that, most of the time, it really doesn't matter, and one can laugh instead of languishing.

...For everyone to whom much is given, from him much will be required; and to whom much has been committed, of him they will ask the more. Luke 12:48

My Super Power is my Energy. A mix of many characteristics that not only make me who I am, but have also has drawn people and continue to draw people to me.

I am aware that because of the value I bring, the impact it makes, the hearts it encourages that much is required of me and, to date, I have barely scratched the surface of what it is that I am required to do in this world. My passion has fired people up, my spirit has lifted others, my aura has made people pay attention, my sensitivity has made me act, my confidence has empowered others, my inspiration has touched hearts, and my humor has made others laugh (or just scratch their heads in wonderment). Understanding the intricacies that make up my Super Power has been an important piece of discovering my purpose and role in this world and will support me as I go and exercise the calling on my life. You, too, have a Super Power. You, too, have a calling. I encourage you to dismantle what makes you who you are and with awareness, run with the vision and make an imprint in this world.

What's Your Super Power

The Comeback is Greater Than the Setback

Feleshia Young

The Comeback is Greater Than the Setback

To whom much is given, much is required. Life throws many curve balls and each one brings on its own share of lessons to be learned. Often times, as I drudged through the vicissitudes of life, I pondered why. Why is this happening to me? Why am I the one who has to endure this? It didn't matter what it was. Whether it was thoughts and feelings of being unloved as a child or having to be a single parent as an adult, the question remained the same, **Why? Why me? Why now? Why am I the only one? Why is God allowing this? Why is God not rescuing me? Why?** In time I learned that with each of the many obstacles and traps sent from Satan himself to destroy my destiny, something was happening to me. Each time I was victorious and even when it seemed as if I failed, I was strengthened because I am God's child and I have power. God had gifted each of us with special gifts. There is a power, a superpower, in you that is greater than anything sent to destroy you. My superpower is resilience. Resilience is the capacity to recover quickly from difficulties.

I have always been very competitive and never a quitter. I am the eldest child. My sister was born when I was five years old. Before she came along, the family member closest to my age was my youngest aunt who was seven years older than me. I had no other siblings around, but I was very close with my aunt and my two youngest uncles who were 10 and 11 years older than me. Being the youngest among people that much older meant I had to be tuff. I had to learn on the fly. My uncles taught me to ride a bike on a boys full sized 10-speed bike. I think back on things like that and I laugh. Do you know the determination I had to have? I am 40 years old and I stand a full 5 feet 2 and a half inches tall. Back then I was so short. I literally had to stand up with my shoulder under the cross bar the entire time I rode. Yet, I did it. Because I was determined. Every time I fell, I would get right back up. Back on the bike I go. I didn't want to be left behind. I wasn't going to let a few falls hold me back from going places. I was about five or six years old then.

I didn't realize it then, but something was activated in me. A drive of determination had been awakened. Conquering the task of learning to ride a bike on my own, despite the challenges that came with it, confirmed within me that I could do anything I put my mind to.

Growing up with the mindset of "I can do anything I put my mind to" often got me into trouble. Telling someone with an "I can do anything I put my mind to" attitude that they can't do something automatically motivates them to do the exact thing you just told them was impossible. This character trait can be dangerous for a child to possess and more times than not the child can be labeled as rebellious and stubborn. I know because I was often misunderstood. I often found myself on the receiving end of a stern talking to, someone drilling into my head how important it is to listen and follow directions. While I agreed whole heartedly that listening was important, I disagreed with the notion of just because it hasn't been done before or the person speaking to me couldn't do it that I would not be able to do it as well. It didn't sit well with me. I just couldn't accept the words of someone else's effort and apply them as my own. I wanted to know for myself. As a child, each victorious accomplishment of proving a nay-sayer wrong only affirmed in me that I should not listen to the "I can't" people of the world, which was great, but as I got older the stern talking was replaced with bumps on the head and set-backs. As you can imagine, a determined child like myself will grow into a pretty head strong teenager.

Adolescence brings on its own set of challenges and my "I can do anything I put my mind to" attitude didn't help at all. Ninth grade at Istrouma High School presented many new opportunities. I have always had a strong belief in God. In high school, I spent my Friday night singing in churches across the state of Louisiana. I was a member of The Students Against Drug Abuse (SADA) choir. I was the average teenager "green" and presumptuous. Boys were becoming more and more interesting. It was 10th grade year and there was this guy in my English class that I found more interesting than all the rest. He never failed to acknowledge my presence and if I missed class, he noticed. I liked that he noticed. Little by little a fondness of him was growing. One day, he wrote me a letter telling me I was beautiful and smart. He told me he liked me and wanted me to be his girlfriend. We dated for the next three years of high school. We had plans to get married when we graduated. I was on cloud nine. I had my whole life planned out. We were going to have two kids. I was going to get my degree in education and become a teacher. He was going to be a band director and we were going to live happily ever after. Unfortunately, things didn't go "perfectly" as I had planned. See, I had not planned for the attention the ring brought from other girls in the school. Looking back, I don't think he did either. Nevertheless, this ring immediately increased his popularity and the rumors started flowing. However now the rumors were constant. People would bring information to me. I would bring it to him. He would deny it. I believed it (as even now I shake my head at myself) and the cycle would start again. Why did I keep believing him? Because he loved me… he would never risk losing me for those girls. I was special. I wore his letterman jacket. He was going to be my first. We were going to live happily ever after. There is no room for cheating in "happily ever after." Then one day there was a rumor that didn't go away. This particular rumor had a life of its own. It would be addressed and then come back up again. The girl attached to this rumor, all of a sudden, became bold. She would walk by his locker while we were there. He would mean mug her and she would keep it moving, but now I was starting to get that uneasy feeling in my gut. Something was going on. I kept asking questions. He kept lying. Until one day he showed up to school with a red mark on his neck. He tried to hide it. He tried to lie about it with the most ridiculous lie ever told. He told me his sister was vacuuming the curtains and the hose fell on his neck. Of course, I didn't believe him. For the first time in my life I was crushed. This was my life, right? I had built my future around this relationship. If it ended, then my future ended, or so I thought. So, after many tears and lies, I decided to stay in the relationship. Nevertheless, I stayed, and he promised that nothing like that would ever happen again. I believed him. I know what you're thinking, but remember, I was 16 years old. Some you all are the age you are now, still believing lies like this. It is my desire that after reading this, you will discover or rediscover the power within you and stop giving it over to someone else. One day, I hear loud talking in the hallway, so of course I listen. Well it turns out the loud talking was directed to me. I don't remember exactly what all was said that day, but the last thing I do remember before I walked out there was her saying, "and I don't care that she is right there in that classroom." Well it turns out that she and my boyfriend were arguing. I walk to the door and she said something to me. I went straight for her head. My math teacher grabbed me and some-how she, the girl was able to bite me in my face. I now have a permanent mark on my face, and that is detrimental to me. It's nothing compared to the scar forming on my heart which at the time I am unaware is forming. Needless to say, I stayed with him. The butterflies I once felt in my tummy when I thought of him had been replaced with uneasiness and anxiety. The security I once felt was under attack unannounced to me. Most of us can't pin-point the exact moment of the first attack on our security because it happens subtly. In fact, I didn't fully realize how much that experience shaped the rest of my life until I was writing this story. I stayed with him through graduation, holding on to what I thought was a powerful love, but in fact it was the love I had for the image I had. At the age of 18 I became pregnant. This pregnancy was shocking to many, including myself. Remember I was the honor roll, SADA choir, church on Friday nights and Sunday mornings teenager with a 10:00 curfew on weekends. I was so afraid to tell my parents that I wrote a letter to my mom and my dad heard about it before I could gather up enough nerve to tell him. My parents were extremely disappointed, and I felt every drop of it. My mom was disappointed because she felt embarrassed. She felt like she failed as a parent. My dad was disappointed that I couldn't come to him and he had to "hear it in the streets." I felt like I let my dad down. He always believed in me. He always had my back. At the same time, my grandmother, my dad's mom, was battling cancer and the union between my mom and dad was rocky to say the least. There was so much pressure in a moment that was designed to be beautiful and celebrated. Many felt I made a great mistake and that my life was ruined. Some even suggested I have an abortion. Maybe in this situation their lives would be ruined, but I was not killing my baby. My attitude was that I will do whatever it takes. **Whatever I have to do to make sure my baby was successful; I was going to do it.** So, against the direction and advice of many, I made the decision I wanted to make. I became a teenage parent. Simultaneously, my grandmother's condition worsened, and my dad begin to struggle with substance abuse. My grandmother passed away just before my son was born. Shortly after he was born, my parents split up. This would be the first time my mother would be on her own. Initially we moved in with my grandmother (my mom's mom), in a two-bedroom house. Including my son that made 5 people in a two bedroom. My aunt that was seven years older than me moved in and we became roommates. This worked for about a year and a half. But then she decided she was going to move back with my grandmother. My mom had gotten her own apartment so there was one free room there. I couldn't afford the bills on my own, so I had to move as well. So here I am, a little over two years after I decided I was going to be a teenage mother, moving back in with my grandmother. I felt like an enormous burden on her. She never said anything to that effect though. She loved having all of us there with her. My son was her first great-grand and she spoiled him rotten I had completed the Medical Assisting program at Camelot College, but it wasn't enough. I always felt like there was more for me.

When my son was two, I met a man. He was seven years older, but he seemed to understand me. He was interesting and fun. He was concerned about my needs as well as the needs of my son. And for the first time in about 5 years, I felt butterflies again. Things moved quickly between us. Within three months of knowing me he bought me a car and helped me get an apartment. After about a year or so he bought a house. Needless to say, I was in love! It's him. Its "Prince Charming" and this is my happily ever after. Let me plan out the rest of our lives together. Are you seeing the pattern yet? Anyway, planning out the rest of our lives meant making it official and getting married. But we couldn't get married because he was already married. He was "separated". About 3 months in the house I noticed "rules" being introduced. I wasn't concerned, I just thought he really cared about us. As time went on the reigns were becoming tighter. I now had to call before I left the house to report everywhere, I went. Disagreements became shouting matches and I felt like a child being scolded by their parent. Of course, I could hold my own in an argument and I did just that. Until that one day we were going back and forth and out of nowhere, wham! Did he just hit me? I was so shocked. I didn't know whether to scream, cry, or call the police. I decided to hit him back. That was the beginning of about six years of physical and verbal abuse. He would come into the house and start a fight about anything. There were so many times I couldn't go to family functions because I had to hide black eyes and bruises all over my body. I have been backhanded in the mouth, punched and slapped so much in the car that I jumped out on the interstate, and threatened if I ever leave, he would find me and kill me. Occasionally I built up the courage to leave only to allow him to make a bunch of empty promises and suck me back in or threaten me. I was so desperate I prayed, "God let this end peacefully. I don't want anyone else to be hurt. Get me out God and I promise I will build an altar to you right here." God did just that.

As you might well imagine that relationship left me battered and bruised not just physically but mentally and emotionally as well. I had no idea who I was anymore. With each disappointment and each let down, I lost a little of myself until there was almost nothing left.

It is often said that the difficult moments in life are the things that mold us into who we are. I disagree. I believe it is the power or superpower we recognize in our ability to recover from difficulties.

It is toughness and the ability to spring back into shape. You see as a child I seemed to be aware of this ability. I didn't have the proper name for it, but I had the confidence I needed to draw on it. As I got older, I begin to give that confidence away. I had more confidence in what another person brought to my life than in myself and my abilities. In high school I had faith and focus in God. He was number one. When I allowed other people and things to have that number one spot, everything in my life went haywire. It was only when I came to myself and put God back into that number one spot in my life did things start to get on track again. I made a promise to God and I never forgot it. He saved me. When I was at the darkest point in my life, he rescued me and loved me back to health. If you are reading this and you think that you are too far gone and God doesn't want you, I'm here to tell you that is a lie. God's love is unconditional. He wants the opportunity to show up in your life just like he did for me. I promised God that if he rescued me, I would build an altar to him. That altar is a non-profit organization I founded dedicated to helping women and children who have been abused or victims of domestic violence. My purpose is to empower women to realize they too possess a great power inside. God has blessed me to obtain a doctorate degree and own a successful counseling practice. He did it for me and I want others to know he can do the same for them. God has gifted each of us with great gifts. It is the challenges of life that will reveal to us what we have on the inside. Romans chapter 5 verses 4-5 NLT says it like this, "And endurance develops strength of character, and character strengthens our confident hope of salvation. And this hope will not lead to disappointment. For we know how dearly God loves us, because he has given us the Holy Spirit to fill our hearts with his love." I absolutely love what I do. When

I hear people talk about surviving or overcoming, I get excited. **I know that each time I am given the opportunity to overcome a challenge in my life my capacity expands.** I'm not backing down from an opportunity just because it looks too hard. I know who I am and who's I am. I am a child of God and you are too. With God, all things are possible. So, don't wait another minute. Pick yourself up and begin the journey to discovering who you are and the power you possess.

What's Your Super Power

The Jewel Within

Dionne Smith

The Jewel Within

S he looked deep within her heart and found a gem, a jewel if it were, a hidden treasure. She had no clue that the gem God gave her from her youth would be the very thing she would use as a weapon to gain strength, to get through obstacles, to navigate through the painful woes of human deception. She didn't discover her secret weapon until she reached the age of maturity. She only uses it when necessary afraid to waste its potent sword. Here's my story.

My super power has given me the strength needed to be rational in times of confusion and it's helped me to understand people when I was disappointed by their actions. My super power is uncommon, it's quiet, subtle, wise, and yet forceful. If not handled properly it can mask itself as the ability to deal with difficult people and accept painful situations willingly. My super power is RESILIENCE. I told you it wasn't conventional. I know that resilience isn't something you can physically see or touch, but once discovered you realize its power and beauty. According to the google dictionary, resilience is the capacity to recover quickly from difficulties; toughness. Can you identify with the definition? Think about your life, reminisce on the obstacles, trials, tribulations you've been through. I'm sure this definition fits you too like a glove. The power of being resilient gets overlooked. We often only associate resilient when we or others are faced with traumatic events and they seemingly recover from it. I had initially attached the word resilience with children who experienced great suffering and survived, but then I realized that resilience was a part of the fabric of every single person I ever met. It wasn't until I recalled my life from childhood until now when I realized that resilience was in my DNA. I wore it like a second skin but didn't know it, nor did I understand it.

Let's explore the word for a second. The origin of the word resilience comes from a Latin word residentia/residere which means "remain". So when I think of resilience and its origin I define it as the ability to remain, being steadfast although life has thrown difficulties, obstacles, heartbreak and disappointment. It's an unwavering internal push and power that whispers in your ear, "girl listen, this may hurt now and you feel like there is no hope … but baby you are going to bounce back from this place. You are going to rise higher, love harder, be more intentional and focused, after this you are going to fully walk in your purpose more powerful than ever before, so do quit, don't give up, don't let go, so gently go through the journey of this pain and watch how you will look on the other side".

Growing up in a strict religious culture I adopted the "be a people pleaser" mindset. I didn't want to be the disruptive child or the problem child. From my youth I desired to please God and my family. I had heavy convictions. My convictions were so heavy I got lost in identifying what I wanted and what others wanted for me. Hearing over and over again about the strong hand of God separated me from identifying his mercy and forgiveness. There were countless preached sermons about living the straight and narrow and I so desperately wanted to be on that path. I literally couldn't imagine straying from it. That said, I wasn't perfect but I definitely wasn't adventurous. I wasn't a risk taker and I longed for the "traditional" white picket fence life style, college, marriage, children and God with no problems or heart break. Well as you can imagine God had a different plan for my life which included love, heartbreak, deception, triumphs, failures, and victories. During my school age years, I didn't meet my super power in its truest form. It wasn't until my first heart break in college. I realized that although the sting of the breakup felt endless I eventually stopped feeling overwhelming hurt. I then fell in love and married in my early 20's but was met with an unfathomable truth that the marriage wouldn't last for 50 yrs like I'd hoped. I was crushed. Although a beautiful daughter was birthed out of the marriage the sting of being a single parent and divorced in my 20's after doing everything the "right" way was catastrophic. I felt like my whole world was crashing in. I felt desperate, alone, and sad beyond belief. Truth be told, I felt disappointed by God. You see, I was always told that if you do things the pure way God will honor your marriage. The faith and religion that I held onto for dear life had failed me "so I thought". The same people who told me that I would live that "perfect picket fence life" if I walked the straight and narrow way were the same people who looked at me with some shame and awkwardness when the marriage dissolved. I felt alone. I was confused about who I was and I surely didn't think I would ever come through it. There I was in a one bedroom apartment that he and I touched in and loved each other in, created our daughter in, left alone to figure life out on my own. I remember holding my 2yr old daughter in my arms night after night and weeping. I truly didn't know how I would ever be "normal" again. I didn't know how the heaviness of the pain would stop. My mind was cloudy and full of questions I couldn't ask anyone but God. I wasn't only emotionally grieved but I was financially worried. I was forced to call my father and ask if me and my daughter could move back into his home. I felt like a complete failure. You see I come from two generations of long lasting marriages, grandparents married over 50yrs and then my parents were married over 20yrs. I was the good and saved little evangelist who failed in relationships. I always thought of myself as lovable, fun, friendly and dedicated. I never would have imagine in a million years that divorce was the journey that would introduce me to my super power.

In the process of moving back into my parents' home with my daughter I prayed a specific prayer. It was a quiet and intense prayer that I didn't even open my mouth to pray it. I used every single ounce of inner mental and emotional strength I had left to pray to my God. **I prayed, "Lord be a husband to me and a father to my daughter".** There was something about that specific prayer that I felt like the heavens heard me. Almost like God was waiting to hear from me. This prayer had nothing to do with her father being a "bad" Dad because he wasn't at all. He remained a good father to our daughter. The prayer was more about asking God to now cover us as I felt naked spiritually and emotionally. I felt uncovered. I'm sure by now you're asking yourself where the super power was. It was in this moment that inner super power started to reveal its beauty, wisdom and peace to me. As the days went on and some time passed my tears lessened, my mind grew clearer, and I felt stronger. You see, I started to feel my authentic self-returning, but I could also feel that I was different. I wasn't green and naïve any longer. The feeling of wanting to please others over myself started to decrease.

107

I began to search within to redefine who I wanted to be and what I wanted out of life. When I started the search I felt something on the inside evolving. I felt something growing inside of my spirit that I couldn't put my finger on. It felt like a push of power, energy, mixed with reassurance and faith. In my search of myself and the discovery of resilience I found a town house that was around the corner from my job. My job opened a daycare in walking distance of my new home, and I applied to get into graduate school and change my career from business to psychology. I remember thinking of where I was, broken and defeated to where God took me too hopeful and at peace. It was right in that moment I met my inner gem, my God given jewel, so wise and so bold. I met Resilience. I embraced it like a longtime friend I had not seen in years. I inhaled the wisdom with every single breath in my body. I felt like there was a security in resilience that I couldn't get from humans. To know that no matter what I go through and what I would experience in life, my super power, my inner "SHERO" resilience would constantly remind me that I could get through anything.

There is so much power in knowing that although life doesn't always seem fair and sometimes we want God to change his decision there is a hope that we will triumph in everything. It reminds me of the scripture in 2 Corinthians 4:8-18 We are troubled on every side, yet not distressed, we are perplexed, but not in despair, Persecuted, but not forsaken, cast down, but not destroyed. This scripture reminds us that the inner resilience God has given us will always accompany us in every single thing we go through. Isaiah 40:31 states, "but they that wait upon the Lord shall renew their strength; they shall mount up with wings as eagles; they shall run, and not be weary, and they shall walk, and not faint." In this scripture it seems as if resilience comes to those that wait on the Lord. After doing some research I found that, the waiting implies the "expectant attitude of faith". I interpret that to mean when we put our trust and faith in our capable God through faith he will cause a renewed strength (Resilience) with intense fierceness, boldness, speed, and persistence. In essence, **God reminds us through his word that there isn't anything that we have to endure that he will not help us through.** There is nothing that he will not guide you through and nothing that he will not strengthen you through. In Isaiah 41:10 it says Fear thou not: for I am with thee, be not dismayed for I am thy God; I will strengthen thee, yea I will help thee yea, I will uphold thee with the right hand of my righteousness. When we are at our lowest point in life, when we are experiencing our hardest trial we have so much fear which at times manifest itself as anger. This scripture reminds us to fear not because he will always hold us up, he will always help us. Like a loving father to his beautiful daughter God will help us while we struggle through life's trials and tribulations.

If there is one lesson I want you to get from this is **you will recover from anything life throws at you**. The super power called resilience will always remind you that the life's trials you overcome in the past will be the shoulder you stand upon for strength. Your resilience, the ability to recover will be the catalyst for your success in your career and relationships. Just like a mother who experiences the physical pain of child birth. Natural labor is excruciatingly painful yet women around the world continue to give birth naturally over and over again. If you're a logical thinker you may say, "Why would anyone endure that level of pain multiple times?". The answer is, resilience. That woman understands that if I made it through my last labor then I will make it through this one. She didn't allow the labor pain to cloud the joy and happiness of the outcome. She understood that the process was worth the promise. So I encourage you to **embrace resilience and inhale its wisdom**. When the storms of life approach you remember there's an inner gem, a jewel, a force given by God that will strengthen you to recover, restore, and rebuild.

My favorite scripture, Psalm 27:13-14 *"I had fainted, unless I had believed to see the goodness of the Lord in the land of the living. Wait on the Lord; be of good courage, and he shall strengthen thine heart: wait, I say on the Lord.*

What's Your Super Power

JUMP!

Erin Porche'

JUMP!

E verything we need is already within us; it's just a matter of making the time and the moves to tap into it. In life, we must Jump!

I jump because I am Kingdom Territory, an heir to the throne of God and a heaven-bound believer who lives a purposed filled life here on earth. God marked stamped me for His ultimate purpose, and my life quest is to fulfill destiny in its totality.

Knowing who I am and whose I am have been key elements of my spiritual DNA and is reflected in my why's, when's, and how's. Jumping, for me, is equivalent to activating my faith. As a child, my family introduced me to the work of God. I believed in His words as I saw His work and incredible power operating in the lives of many in the Bible, and others around me. Believing in God's word gave me the confidence to stand on it, walk in it, and JUMP. In life, I was led to jump off the porch as a teen mom, fresh out of high school, deciding that I would not just be another statistic. I decided that I would change the narrative of my family's history. I graduated summa cum laude with aspirations to be valedictorian. Education was everything to me; it was my outlet from the realities at home and the environment I lived in.

Expectations were always high, and me giving birth to a child in my junior year of high school was not included in the long list of expectations. From the good, bad, and ugly, I had perspective and information that led me as I journeyed through life. My foundation was solid, being built on things eternal and according to the word of God. So, I jumped making choices and decisions in life, career, and business in season.

I targeted jobs, enrolled in specialized training sessions, traveled to different communities, and enrolled them in the best schools. As a Practitioner of life and business, I jumped, knowing everything I needed was already within me or accessible to learn and apply... I believed I could achieve knowledge for everything I needed to know to get through life by making the time to seek out the information. I was always blessed to build relationships, connect the dots, and work my way up and out. I was intentional about serving top leaders that ultimately poured so much value into me. I have also been blessed to have a natural ability to bring people and ideas together in innovative ways. I never wasted energy fighting the inevitable. The serenity prayer has been a part of my life for as long as I can remember. I always felt as if reciting it, made my life flow freely. God's word is deeply rooted in my soul, and it has been a guiding compass and a source of peace for me to jump and make a move in life and business. The serenity prayer has taught me how to respond to tough times and encourage me to remember that I serve a bigger God than all difficulties, setbacks, and missteps. God has always been there to take care of all of it, no matter what "it" is.

I have always trusted my gut and tapped into the power that God bestows upon me. I firmly believe that God created us in His image and made His strength available to us. He said in His words that He would never leave us nor forsake us. We are never alone, no matter how hard things may get. I believe His word because He said that if He called me to "it," whatever "it" was, no matter how high up it seemed, I would always JUMP, and He would lead the way. In the beginning, seeing was believing for me, and it made me have faith that things were within reach and attainable. The word and works of God ignited my faith to see beyond what eyes can see in the natural. It moved me to believe that God moves in the spiritual realm, and that makes me eager to JUMP. My superpower is jumping. Therefore, I am never stagnant. This is a perpetual posture I seek to flow in my daily life. Having faith to leap in an upward and forward motion, seeking higher heights spiritually, personally, and professionally, has blessed my life. I'm never 100% sure of where I may land, but having the faith to move, and jump, has served me well. It has brought me to a place of elevation and Life mastery.

When I jump, I position myself to make a move. I have prayed and consulted God and situated myself to trust the process, whatever it may be. I have also assessed the situation, looking at the good, bad, and ugly. I have evaluated the risks and what-ifs with wisdom. I learned that seeking counsel from God and waiting to hear from Him is vital to my life every step of the way. Knowing God is with me gives me the faith to JUMP.

Hurdles faced when Jumping.

The mechanics of jumping is fascinating to me. The height of your jump depends on the power in your muscles and your center of gravity. It has been found that the lower you go, the more stable you become. This, for me, has proven to be a fact on more than one level. As a Christian in the Kingdom of God, when I humble myself or become low, I garner strength from God. His power fills me up and enables me to do things I would not be able to do otherwise. When I have God as my center, I can JUMP higher than I ever could if there was something else in His place.

Hardship and adversity bring me down low as well. When going through rough times, sometimes I feel so low that I'm quite sure I'm flat on my face, grounded and prostrate before God. However, just like science dictates, the lower I get, the higher I can JUMP. Henceforth, the bounce-back effect in life has exceeded my imagination with God's work of elevation.

I used to allow relationships with men to distort my center of gravity and through me off balance instead of becoming grounded. Misplaced values with men separated me from getting close to God. Childhood sexual trauma contributed to my lack of self-worth and impacted my self-perception. It distorted my ability and willingness to adhere to the principles of the Bible. It also colored my ideas of how much I chose to submit to men. I acted like a wife to men that I was never married to, enslaved to the relationship. It was a conscious decision, as I believed that it was all I needed for my life. But God grew me from such toxic and warp perceptions and imbalances in relationships with a companion. This was a growth process of more than 30 years of my life.

Whether they were amazing relationships or physically and mentally toxic ones, I always grew from them. From heartbreak to divorce, I am now at a point in life where I know who I am. I know what I desire in my relationship and possess a healthier perspective of the values and traits that should exist in life-partnership. After my divorce, I chose to be celibate, and in this process, I experienced freedom. My relationships today are well balanced with communication and healthy boundaries.

Gratefully, I have always maintained a growth mindset. I decided that as long as I had breath in my body,

I would continue to learn, expand my reach, and change for the better. I naturally became adaptable, which served me well as I often found myself navigating my way through crises.

My up-brining and my faith always led me right back to God. After I experienced hurt, undesired results, and losses that all grew and expanded my life portfolio, God was always there. Every time I returned to God's arms, He placed me back on the track of my divine destiny.

Jumping is a choice, attitude, and posture. It requires the willingness to spring into action and move from one stage to the next. In my own journey, I've had to spring into action and get moving without prior notice. As a result, I have been able to master the art of traveling, transitioning, and connecting with people in various environments with different backgrounds.

Jumping has always been rooted in transition. I had to master transitions early in life. I attended six different elementary schools and lived in more houses than I can recall. This exposed me to different environments and helped me to appreciate diversity. I have learned to be flexible and comfortable with ever-changing conditions and become more secure in my identity. I have an innate ability to generate ideas and provide sound advice to others. Life and business mastery is the space I connect and help the most people.

I can jump despite uncertainties. I can move because I place my trust and confidence in God, and I know that I will always come out victorious on the other end. I have what it takes to thrive in any environment because the Creator of the universe dwells inside me.

I believe what the word says about there being a season for everything. I know that seasons will change, so a part of my ministry helps others deal with the ever-shifting seasons of life. I empower and guide them to come out of every situation, victorious.

When I focus on God's power and obey His voice, and His leadership, I feel empowered. I tap into the promise of Philippians 4:13 that I can do all things through Christ's strength, and I feel fearless. I feel like I'm walking and moving under God's divine order and acting according to His strength.

I have always walked in authority and wanted abundance for my life. I believe these thoughts are rooted in my mind and contributed significantly to the results I have been blessed with. I believe that if we claim God's promises, we are already there and equipped to walk in faith and power.

Faith and obedience are keys to walking in purpose. Understand and seek God in prayer, then wait on Him. This formula has carried me through many challenging days. It has taken me down to a crouching position of worship and built the springboard from which I willingly JUMP. I have always experienced God giving a glimpse of His glory, and fragments of the story. My faith in the completion of the work that God has begun in me keeps me JUMPING. I thank God for giving me the gift of discernment and foresight. They have been my portion and enabled me to activate my superpower. No matter what the results are, I jump higher and further because I know in whose hands I will land.

I believe every woman should identify with this experience because we are supreme beings. We are masterpieces created by the Master and God did not create us with a spirit of fear, but of power, love, and a sound mind. As women, we are blessed with the gift of bringing life into the world. With such responsibility, we must be decisive and MOVE. We must be prepared to JUMP because someone is counting on us to do just that. Jumping requires faith and trust in God. Every woman should also know and trust that God is the source of every aspect of life. If we follow His divine order and everything we do and say is in keeping with his word, He will bless us according to His will. God will grant us the desires of our hearts, which includes our husbands. When we walk in God, He will send us a true man of God, made in His image. This man will be worthy of our honor, trust, and submission. Additionally, we would be equipped to live our purpose-driven life transitioning and flowing in a vein of power and influence, jumping, floating, and flying in full grace, experiencing a life full of glory.

A personal relationship with God is vital. It is as important as the air we breathe. God created us, and everything we are is rooted in him. Growing to know Him connects us to our roots. Understanding that the very air in our lungs is God-given, and the blood flowing through our veins flows from Jesus, is a necessity to having a relationship with Him. Honestly, I would be lost without

God. There were times I was lost and had gone far from God. Looking back on those times now, I realize that I was off the path with no sense of navigation, vision, or visibility. I was reminded that only God could give me the gift of foresight. This way of life is personal and requires relationship, submission, conversation, intimacy, and understanding. All the fruits of the spirit are vital to a relationship with God, and will only come from this relationship.

Maintaining this position and posture has kept me in a place of abundance and blessings. My relationship with God is a daily walk and talk. In the same way that earthly relationships require consistent communication to be strengthened, our spiritual connection does as well. God does not need us to talk to Him so that He can be "more God," but we need to be with Him to be more like God.

I want the readers to be empowered and activated to JUMP, trust, and believe God's promises for their life, and live it out loud. When I realized that God wanted to use my story for His glory, I began to make declarations. I want everyone to know that you can have it all if you seek God first in all things and allow Him to perfect, protect, and prevail in your life. Know that you are victorious and walk in it. Walk boldly in the transactional promise of Matthew 6:33, "But seek ye first the kingdom of God, and his righteousness; and all these things shall be added unto you."

I want the reader to decree and declare:

I will let it be known that I know who and whose I am, so I will jump!

Everything I need is already within me!

I am living in a decade of dominion!

I am a warrior, so I will jump!

I am bold, so I will jump!

I have a purpose, so I will jump!

My DNA is royalty, so I will jump!

My purpose is profound, so I will jump!

I am decisive, so I jump!

I live with winning principles, so I jump!

I know God is intentional, and I am proof that His grace is sufficient, so I will jump!

I forgive my enemies and release all hurt and pain and give them to God, so I will be free to jump!

I trample and tread upon serpents, so I can jump!

I have a sound mind of God, so I jump!

My Voice will be used to spread words of wisdom for generations to come!

I will face it and replace it, so I will jump!

I testify to serve notice on the enemy!

I walk daily under the covering of God's amazing grace and tender mercy!

The blood gives me strength and power to accomplish everything He has called me to do!

I will boldly and loudly profess the word and work of God!

I trust God's word to add all things unto me, and I know all means ALL!

There will be no lack!

I am the blueprint, and when I jump, I will fly and flow freely!

My decree and declaration establish me as Kingdom Territory!

Therefore, with theses decrees and declarations, I will JUMP. I will DO IT Boldy and freely with no regret!

My favorite scripture is 1 John 4:7-21, "I am love, and I live and walk in total love for all humanity." I am Lady Erin Love.

What's Your Super Power

Resilience.

To know that no matter what I go through and what I would experience in life my supper power my inner sherio resilience would remind me that I could get through anything

A Mother's Cry

Tosha Mills

A Mother's Cry

"Mothers and their children are in a category all on their own. There's no bond so strong in the entire world. No love so instantaneous and forgiving." -Gail Tsukiyama, Dreaming Water

If you ask any mother what is most important to her, she will respond with absolute conviction "my children." Where would our children be without their mothers? For most of us, we are the foundation of our households. We are made to push through obstacles without breaking down while continuously trying to make the breakthrough. **We are fearless and bold.** We are the lifelong cheerleaders. We are made to be strong and build our children with an aptitude for success and without limitations. We are nurturers and heroes. Regardless of what happens in our own lives, we always persevere and move forward. When we are sick, we simply medicate ourselves with no complaint to others. If we have moments of fear or weakness, we go to an area where no one sees us. In that spot, we let out a big sigh, have a cry, stand up, and push through despite never knowing what lies ahead. When our hearts break, and we are engulfed with pain, the only person that truly knows what we are going through is God. Being a mother is the greatest job in the world, but it is also an endless job. Despite all of this, mothers are not perfect.

While mothers inspire dreams and possibilities, there are wounds and misfortunes along the way. No one ever told mothers that such wounds and misfortunes would leave crushed inside suffering massive amounts of pain. No matter the pain, mothers will endure it because of the immense love for our children. Mothers are educators, disciplinarians, confidantes, and best friends to their beloved children. When the unexpected happens, our painful heartbreak runs deeper than any abyss of darkest oceans. The pain of our children will always overshadow the pain of our own past.

As mothers, our duty is to not only hear our children but to listen to them. There will be things we are excited to hear and we celebrate. Unfortunately, there are also things that will bring us to our knees with a sorrowful reality intimidating our souls. Repeatedly, there will be times we must mute our voices even when we have so much to say so we may listen to our children. Our children need to have a voice and, as mothers, we know this is a necessary part of their growth. As much as we try to prevent any pain from harming our children, we are also aware that there will be times we cannot prevent such sorrow. During those times, we must stand firm that God will fix all unimaginable events … even if we do not bring them to him.

Mothers give life to their children with a love so beautiful there is no scholar that can define it. Mothers can also chip away life with their own thoughts, actions, and ever-changing experiences. In our life shattering moments, we cry rivers. Some of us have been raped, beaten, and brutally broken; yet, we rise. We usually stand in silence, because that is what we are taught. That is what I was taught, anyway. Even now, I can hear my mom in Heaven saying, "What goes on in my house, stays in my house." The excruciating hardships that I encountered in that very house have been tucked away in

Pandora's Box never to be discussed again. This is a repeated philosophy.

What happens when we remain silent within ourselves never sharing Pandora's Box with others? We develop an ever-growing sickness that festers and permanently sticks to the depths of our being forever changing our core. Despite our best effort, this sickness never stays locked away forever. It shows its ugly face during our trials and tribulations like some sort of cruel reminder of how bad things can be. What's worse is this cruel sickness passes onto our children, their children, and so on.

As a mother of a son who is spending what should have been the best years of his life in a prison cell, my natural desire is to be there for him by way of visits and making sure that he has what he needs. In an earlier writing, my son mentioned how "we let each other down." This was the hardest thing for me to accept as I had considered myself to be a good mother. Suddenly, I realized that I had actually let him down in ways that my mother had let me down. Like so many of us, we submerse ourselves in our careers dismissing things we consider unimportant. It is later when we realize those "unimportant" things were actually important cries from our children screaming "I need you." It is then our sickness reminds us of that all too familiar feeling of what it feels like to have our cries ignored. Like I said, Pandora's Box is never locked forever.

Our children have no idea what it's like to be a mother. Our first instinct is to work, so we may provide for their needs. Even with the best intentions, we sometimes fail. I can almost hear so many of you mumbling "not me." But it is you. It happens to all of us. There is no such thing as perfect motherhood. Daily, mothers question themselves about their decisions. Was it the right decision? Did I make the right choice? Will there be unknown consequences as a result of such decisions? Mothers tend to parent with guilt when there is no father figure, which turns out to be one of the biggest mistakes that we can ever make.

Most often, when we give tough love in teaching our children life's hard lessons, we are often called mean. In doing our best to help our children grow, we see them distancing themselves from us in defiance. Little do they understand how much they hurt us and bring us to tears. Little do they understand that regardless of our own feelings, we will continue to stand firm for if we don't, we know we will do more harm than good. Children have no clue what it's like to be a mother. The truth is, at their age, we didn't have a clue either.

I do not claim to be a therapist nor a trained professional. I am sharing my own experiences, mistakes, struggles, and triumphs with you in the hope that you will realize you are not alone. You are not the only one going through life's journey. While the path we are on may differ, the journey is filled with much of the same trials and tribulations. We share a common denominator: we are all mothers on the quest to becoming a better parent. **One thing that remains true regardless of any circumstances is that a mother's love is a love that never waivers and lives forever.**

What's Your Super Power

About the Authors

Nadia Lindsey Francois, native of Baton Rouge, Louisiana is a serial entrepreneur with a heart for people. A hairstylist by trade, Nadia holds current licenses in Cosmetology and Barbering and a B.S. in Business Administration. She began her entrepreneurial journey at the age of 19 and has used her experiences and knowledge to help other business owners start and grow their businesses. Nadia's number one assignment is being the mother and sole provider for her four sons, the driving force behind her persistent hustle and diligent pursuit of greatness. She is the Founder and Executive Director of Sistars of Empowerment, Inc a nonprofit that focuses on empowering, educating and inspiring women and the youth in Baton Rouge and the surrounding areas. In February 2013, Nadia decided to pursue her dream of giving back and established a platform that provides tools for enhancing knowledge, life skills and entrepreneurship. She uses her life experiences along with the outreach of other mentors and professionals to empower our women and children to

What's Your Super Power?

become successful, confident, self-sufficient members of society. She is a trailblazer who has developed a series of programs and workshops that contribute to personal and entrepreneurial growth. Under Nadia's leadership, SOE grew from what started off as a group of friends wanting to give countless acts of community service has now grown into a thriving sisterhood that incorporates motivational and business workshops, youth confidence and esteem pageants as well as mentorship from Baton Rouge to the Lafayette areas. In August 2018, Nadia became a first time author. She published The Entrepreneur Activity Workbook as her first project which is very close to her heart. She created this workbook to assist entrepreneurs in having a clear business plan and understanding of their business goals. In keeping with her beauty industry roots, in 2019 Nadia launched Heiress Haircare Systems which includes three maintenance products. Edge Tamer, Growth Serum, and Hair Polisher excel in quality and promote healthy hair growth. In three short months, Heiress Haircare Systems expanded into a full line of hair growth and skincare products offered exclusively online and local beauty supply stores. In February 2020, Nadia had the opportunity to teach her fellow beauty and barber colleagues The Power of Entrepreneurship course, "Hustlenomics" at the Bronner Brothers Multi Cultural Beauty Show. Her efforts as a serial entrepreneur continue to excel as God opens more doors and her brand receives more exposure.

Learn more about Nadia and her businesses at

www.heiressint.com

Nicole is a native of Baton Rouge, Louisiana and the eldest of 4 siblings. Nicole's professional career has afforded her the humble opportunity to work closely with people from all walks of life. As a mother, aunt, entrepreneur, and pastor, Nicole is most passionate about providing opportunities for others to advance in their purpose, while developing their passion. As a certified business development consultant, organizational developer, a connector of people and resources, Nicole is the founder and executive director of *The **BR**idge Agency, INC,* a grassroots nonprofit organization serving the East Baton Rouge Parish. As the founder, Nicole links together the relationships she has built over a period of twenty-two (22) plus years within the community and professional background to forge a massive hand on collaborative efforts to empower, advocate and, serve the residents of the city of Baton Rouge, while addressing the social drivers of crime. Nicole is a leader of leaders with an immense passion for improving systems and people through service.

L aurinda Andujar is a Florida native and two-time published author. She is married and the mother of three sons. Her most recent work, She Blinked: The Book of Me was released in October of 2018. She is eagerly awaiting the new release of her new book Confessions of a Serial Dater: To all the boys I never loved in 2020.

Laurinda has been featured in multiple print, radio and television publications, such as Fashion Gxd Magazine, Swagher Magazine, and NBC amongst others. Laurinda is a Certified Grief Recovery Specialist as well as a Certified John Maxwell Team Member and Transformational Leadership Coach.

She is also the founder of SheBlinked LLC, which is a leadership development organization and Heal the City Inc, a charitable organization, which focuses on assisting those attempting to navigate through trauma. With that said, Laurinda has been invited to speak at venues both domestically and internationally. She has a heart for service and has participated in mission trips to South America on numerous occasions and hosts free conferences globally.

Laurinda has been recognized by the National Coalition of 100 Black Women, the National Diversity Council, as well as Barry University and other organizations for acts of service. Laurinda is currently pursuing her Bachelor's degree in Business Management at American Public University. She often jokes that, of all that trauma that she had experienced in life, Microeconomics is the single most traumatic experience to nearly took her out.

http://www.fashiongxxd.com/up-next/2019/4/17/fashion-gxd-magazine-presents-up-next-with-laurinda-andujar

https://www.brproud.com/news/heal-the-city-the-boot-edition-coming-to-baton-rouge-this-summer/

In terms of enhancing beauty and healthy hair, Enola is an expert. As a former graduate of Avoyelles High School (1992), The Academy of Hair Technology (1994), Toastmasters (2017) and Miracle University (2018), she has been leveraging excellence in the beauty industry. Enola also pursued training at Ever Increasing Word Training Center (2017) and increased her career path as a Motivational Speaker in ministry, while obtaining a bachelor's degree in Cosmetology at LSBBA.

Throughout her career, she has attended and participated in multiple hair shows and ongoing trainings across the world. She is dedicated to bringing the latest trends to the beauty industry. Enola strongly believes that continuing education is the key to providing excellent customer service and obtaining success. Enola is a passionate hairstylist with 23 years of experience. She has mastered the gift of creative styles and hair techniques including natural hair, weaving, dreadlocks and updos. She specializes in trendy hair coloring and pixie cuts. Enola provides an environment for integrating beauty and wellness into her styling routine and level of service, ensuring that her clients experience is extraordinary.

Enola is not only an educator, stylist, beauty consultant and workshop facilitator, she is also a life coach and a published author. Enola is the author of the newly acclaimed book, "Adjusting Your Crown," a testimonial story of tragedy and triumph. This book was birth through the struggle of motivating others to pursue their dreams and goals while appearing to be defeated and setback but only to realize that in the end, she overcame and now fulfilling her purpose.

D r. Treva Tarnese Brown grew up in Baton Rouge, Louisiana. She graduated with her Bachelors of Science degree in Chemistry from Louisiana State University in 2011 and continued her education as a doctoral student at the University of New Orleans where she upheld a prestigious Louisiana Board of Regents Graduate Fellowship. She received her Ph.D. in Chemistry in 2017, with a dissertation focus on advanced nano-mechanical investigations and characterizations of layered oxide nanomaterials.

Dr. Brown began her career as a physical scientist in 2018 for the United States Naval Research Laboratory at NASA Stennis Space Center in Mississippi, where she studies microbial corrosion. She is an active member of Alpha Kappa Alpha Sorority, Incorporated, the National Organization of Black Chemists and Chemical

Engineers, the American Chemical Society, and the Microscopy Society of America. Outside the realm of science, she has a passion for dance, travel, unique cuisines, and holds a special place in her heart for mentoring youth. Lastly, Dr. Brown holds the 2020 title of Ms. Black Empowerment Louisiana. Her platform, "You Can Too", is to encourage youth and young adults to attain their goals no matter the obstacles encountered along the way.

With this project, Dr. Brown hopes to encourage others to strive for their goals despite any circumstance. Her motivation to participate in this compilation was to be a voice for young women navigating life and careers. A work such as this gives women the power, motivation, and encouragement to conquer whatever life throws our way.

Tammy Boone (Tammy Raé), is a Certified Training Professional, Certified Life Coach, Public Speaker, Domestic Abuse and Mental Wellness Advocate.

She is a business professional, founder of Tammy Raé - Purposed by Design 365, a sister, an aunt, and a great friend. However, she was trapped by her over-analytical antics and lack of self-confidence.

Tammy Raé had succumbed to the damaging thoughts of yesterday and while she had no clue what the future held, she was certain that she did not want to remain detained in her past. As a result, she silenced her inner critic and begin working on herself. In doing so, she *discovered her worth.* An unearthing that restored many broken pieces which helped her to reconcile years of internal conflict.

Speaking, coaching, writing, mentoring, and community involvement affords her the opportunity to share her formal and experiential lessons of life with humility, transparency, vulnerability, and conviction. She is passionate about reaching women and positioning them to push beyond their "stuck."

Vuyanzi's greatest teacher has been faith. Her passion in life is to help black leading ladies over 40 to discover their greatness after a shift in normalcy. She specializes in working with women who are looking to align their purpose with their soul connected livelihood. She has been called the Queen of Reinvention.

Vuyanzi experienced the alarm clock of destiny in her own life and it ignited her soul to champion her best self. The connection to God and faith empowered her to look deeply into who she was and to take action. She needed clarity to find meaning and intent and this is when she embodied the guidance of faith and spirituality. There was a dynamic re-visioning of her mission and it was a shift; the catalyst to hone her greatness, heal and transform.

Vuyanzi is a black female powerhouse who is laser-focused to awaken and turbo-charge your destiny whether you are transitioning toward retirement, pivoting in your business, or suppressing through a perplexed changeover in your personal life, there is an alarm clock of destiny that is impacting your best self. As your Personal Destiny Coach, she would welcome the opportunity to help you channel that break-through and align your faith with your soul connected path and purpose.

Vuyanzi is Certified Life, Career, Executive Coach, an Inspirational Speaker and an Author.

D r. Feleshia Borskey-Young is a Licensed Professional Christian Therapist, Motivational Speaker, Minister, and visionary. She is a graduate of Istrouma Senior High School in Baton Rouge Louisiana. In April of 2016, Dr. B Young, as she prefers to be called, earned her doctoral degree in Christian Counseling and Biblical Psychology. Dr. Young has since founded Solutions Counseling Services, LLC in Baton Rouge, where she has counseled numerous men, women, children, and married couples back to a healthy place in life. Dr. Young serves as executive director of Women Affairs at Heavenly Hope Ministries in Baker LA, where she administrates the "Queens of Hope Life

Enrichment Program". Dr. B Young is also the Founder of the 411ForWomen Outreach Organization. This organization is dedicated to women and children who have been victims of domestic and intimate partner violence. As a survivor of Domestic Violence and teenage pregnancy, Dr. B Young is passionate about serving the people of God, especially His daughters. Dr. Young understands the courage and support required to overcome such unfortunate and evil circumstances. Her biblically sound knowledge coupled her life's experiences, allows her to relate to and share with believers and non-believers alike. She has accepted her life's assignment to inspire, motivate, and edify others.

Above all her accomplishments Dr. Young considers supporting her husband in ministry and

guiding her children to be valuable assets to Society as her primary purpose. Dr. Young believes this compilation provides yet another opportunity to present the truth and dispel the lies that encourage self-hate, neglected potential, abuse, and unhealthy kingdom marriages.

Dionne Smith is a native of Philadelphia, PA born to Bishop Howard and First Lady Diane Crosby. As a child she was spiritually reared in the National Temple Pentecostal Church of God under the leadership of the Late Bishop Norris Heastie and Paternal Grandmother Pastor Grace L. Crosby. As a youth in ministry Dionne Smith used her gift of servitude by working as a Youth Leader. She sang as a praise and worship leader and acted as a youth community facilitator. Dionne Smith attended Delaware State University and majored in Psychology where she earned her Bachelor of Science undergraduate degree. She furthered her studies at Wilmington College where she received her Masters of Science degree in Community Counseling and was inducted into the Chi Sigma Iota Honors Society. As a woman of God and a Licensed Professional Counselor, with a sincere passion for mending the brokenhearted and bringing healing to the trouble minded, Dionne Smith has provided counseling services, both individual and group settings pertaining to: Family, Individual, Children & Adolescents, Grief, Spiritual, and Substance Abuse. In 2006, Dionne

Smith volunteered at Supporting KIDDS, which provided group grief counseling to children working through death or divorce. Dionne also volunteered as a co-facilitator, in 2008, of a weekly women's codependency and life skills group. In 2010 she was appointed Vice President of W.O.E. (Women of Excellence), a non-profit agency which served domestic violence victims. She continued to be an agent of change serving the mental health population in the communities of Pennsylvania, Delaware, and later on in Louisiana. In 2017, she launched two businesses, Made Whole Counseling, LLC and Motivatemedee which focuses on empowering women, motivational mentorship and providing therapeutic treatment. On September 3, 2011, Dionne Smith, affectionately known as " Lady Dee" was joined in Holy Matrimony to Dr. Bishop Michael Smith Sr. To this union, Dionne Smith is the extremely proud mother of one daughter Victoria (The Diva-College Student) and one son, (The Rambunctious-Drummer) 4yr old Michael II. On June 23, 2018 Dionne Smith was installed as a Pastor. She and her husband co-lead the great churches of New Covenant Christian Center &

Jericho International Ministries. While leading as a mother both naturally and spiritually to many sons and daughters, and maintaining her professional career, she continues to remain faithful and work diligently in her calling. As Dionne Smith strives to display the characteristics of a Virtuous Woman, she stands firmly on the word of God. She desires to be a continued agent of emotional healing and to spread the gospel of Jesus Christ to lost souls worldwide. She believes "I had fainted, unless I had believed to see the goodness of the Lord in the land of the living. Wait on the Lord: be of good courage, and he shall strengthen thine heart: Wait, I say on the Lord". Psalm 27:13-14

Love, Health, and Wellness mind, body, and soul are the key to our wealth and life mastery.

Meet Erin Porche`, commonly known as Lady Erin Love, a growth strategist, and consulting catalyst, who will try anything once. Erin has helped develop and build capacity for leaders in businesses across the nation on a federal, regional, state, and local scale, improving operations and modernizing tools and systems to achieve maximum results and increase their bottom line and profit margins.

As a mother of 3 unorthodox, witty, peculiar children, Erin knows the meaning of love, nurturing, and methods of mastering to multiply. Erin loves to travel, dance, build, and have high vibrating conversations. Erin is a lifelong learner and continues her education and training across multiple industries.

Lady Erin is the CEO and Founder of Global Works Consulting Group, a multinational conglomerate headquartered in Baton Rouge, Louisiana, with global reach. Erin loves to help acquire lucrative business opportunities and crush their goals and dreams in life, ministry, and business.

She is a natural-born innovator, creator, critical thinker, multi-disciplined problem solver, and servant leader with substantial project experience in operations, process improvement, quality management, business continuity, disaster preparedness, prevention, response, recovery, and local engagement.

With over 15 years of executive consulting experience, Lady Erin brings a wealth of experience and knowledge across multiple industries to the table spanning from co-authoring emergency management frameworks and plans, revising policy, creating and presenting training and exercises, to facilitating and coordinating resources among over 50 agencies for special events. Her work specializes in business modernization, problem-solving, solution building, and organizational change management. Clients love her because of her passion, go-getter zeal, and unshakable commitment to helping people of all walks of life recognize their brilliance.

Featured in the Advocate News, WAFB TV, DHS Secretary Corner, Hometown Productions - Broadcasting & Media, MAX 94.1 Radio, Our Minds on Freedom, Baton Rouge Business Report, and YWCA publications. With a wealth of knowledge, diplomatic approach, and systematic thinking, Lady Erin has an unshakable commitment to helping business owners outsource, delegate, and maximize the use of their time to create the life and business that they truly desire.

She builds bridges, offering trusted advice to close the consulting field's gaps by connecting the dots on how to secure contracts and business deals. Erin enjoys connecting people and resources to the suppliers and networks that they need to grow and scale their business with ease.

Lady Erin is a relentless champion of business owners, founders, C-suite executives, and risk-takers. She works tirelessly to empower top-performing leaders to own their success, so they can take risks, get noticed, and create change with confidence.

Lady Erin's knack for details and natural approach to connect with people activates and unlocks the lucrative world of fulfillment in life and business in the marketplace.

Tosha Smith Mills, a native New Orleanian, is a courageous 40-something-year-old (not going to tell her actual age) with almost any life experience that any adult could experience. She is a serial entrepreneur with over fifteen years of experience as CEO of The Talent Connexion, LLC, a successful talent agency in New Orleans, who has placed talent in an extensive list of Hollywood accredited films, television shows, and commercials; Tosha also has over eighteen years of experience in the legal field. Through this, she has discovered her passion in writing and is fulfilled by sharing her testimonies, empowering those in need, and helping others find their life's purpose.

On any given day, you will find Tosha speaking about her life as a Best-Selling and Award Winning Author of "Momma I Should of Listened: A Voice of Pain and Power" which details the horrific and undeniable pain that she encountered after her teenage son was sentenced to 40 years in prison. She will cry with you, inspire you, and motivate you to live the life God has intended for you to live.

Tosha has been on a never-ending speaking tour that has landed her in the same media seats that Jay Z and Denzel Washington sit. Tosha has been a featured guest on The Breakfast Club, Majic102, WYLD FM, The Laura Coates Show, WQUE 93 FM, WWL Radio, The Philipe Matthews Show and several other media outlets. She has also served as speaker/panelist at the Morehouse School of Medicine, John Jay Criminal College in NYC, Sacramento State Prison, along with speaking at several churches, conferences, schools, youth facilities, prisons, and nonprofit organizations.

After a child lands in prison, the parents are always the forgotten piece that leaves a question mark hanging over their head. Often times, the parents are often misunderstood, and judged which leaves them helpless and sometimes even hopeless. Tosha created an organization called Parents with Voices, Inc., that helps to support families through their own personal crisis and teach them how to cope and operate in their freedom.

Tosha is the wife to John, a mother to four young men, Blake, William, Christopher, and Trae, and a source of inspiration to all.

When Tosha is not working, which is rare, she is spending her time traveling, reading, or walking alongside clients on the red carpet.

CPSIA information can be obtained
at www.ICGtesting.com
Printed in the USA
JSHW040512241020
9042JS00002B/5